Pablo's book is interesting to read and we of theological grounding in Scripture tog is a major contribution to the Christian popular particularly since the psychological angle is given.
Dominic Beer, Consultant Psychiatrist and Senior Lecturer working in the NHS and at the University of London, and author of Mad, Bad or Sad: A Christian Approach to Antisocial Behaviour and Mental Disorder

This book will offer great comfort to those whose lives are marked by persistent thorns in the flesh. It provides a rich diet of biblical content, wise pastoral counsel and pertinent advice born from personal experience and deep study of the Scriptures.
Lindsay Brown, former General Secretary, IFES

Pablo is an experienced Christian leader and a practising psychiatrist, and both these strands are evident in this excellent book. It is profoundly biblical, practically helpful, moving and encouraging.
Lady Elizabeth Catherwood

Pablo reflects on his deep experiences as a psychiatrist, Christian leader and fellow sufferer and distils the best of them into this wonderful book. *A Thorn in the Flesh* comprises a unique blend of professional clinical experience along with personal suffering and robust theological reflection. It reveals the remarkable explanatory power and coherence of the biblical world-view, while at the same time offering the reader the transforming power of the gospel of grace. I wholeheartedly commend it.
Reverend Richard Cunningham, Director, UCCF The Christian Unions

Pablo Martinez truly understands the pain that accompanies a thorn in the flesh, and he writes with clarity, conviction and godly wisdom. If you are looking for a way out of discouragement or even despair connected with an affliction in your own life, this short but insightful book will open the door towards a new path of hope and practical help. I highly recommend it!
Joni Eareckson Tada, JAF International Disability Center

The apostle Paul was surely deliberately vague when he did not specify the nature of his 'thorn in the flesh'. Was it a physical or psychiatric illness, a recurring temptation, or a difficult relationship?

Whatever it was, each of us has our own thorn, and Dr Pablo Martinez is the man to help. He writes not just theologically, not just as an experienced psychiatrist, but as someone who has suffered all his adult life from a thorn that God has not taken away.

Pablo brings comfort out of that experience as he points us towards help – towards acceptance, grace, perseverance and hope.

Dr Andrew Fergusson, Head of Communications, Christian Medical Fellowship and author of Hard Questions about Health and Healing

This useful book examines what the Scriptures describe as a 'thorn in the flesh'. It makes a valuable contribution to our understanding of the effects of chronic physical, social and psychological problems on individuals and their communities. The aim is to find personal peace and growth in an irreversible situation through a new understanding of what it all means. Pablo examines carefully what the Scriptures have to say and gives valuable guidance for thinking about the problems in a new way. The fact that he himself has suffered from a chronic physical disability from the age of eighteen adds great credibility to the material – he knows what he is writing about.

The great strength of this book is that it begins with the author's personal account and ends with testimonies that outline in narrative form how both the person and the supporters in the community learned how to accept the situation and find some sort of positive meaning in it.

Before the final testimonies there are six useful chapters. These lead the reader to a new understanding of the enemy of our faith, to pathways to acceptance of the problem, and finally to a new understanding of God's grace and the strength of weakness. They are full of biblical and experiential teaching, culminating in the thorn turning into something quite different – a new way of relating to God. In conclusion, a useful glossary of medical terms and a substantial reference list are provided.

There is such a wealth of detail in this book that initially I needed to write a summary of the sub-headings in each chapter, but I ended up by realizing that I had learned something that will be useful to me in my relationship with sick people and their communities for the rest of my life.

Marjory F. Foyle, consultant psychiatrist to international missions

After carefully analysing what constitutes a 'thorn' in our experience, and the various ways we can react to such, Martinez accepts our instinct to ask: 'Why? Why me?' He explains to us our need to learn to 'fix our gaze on the stars' in the darkness of the night of suffering, in the midst of the storms of life. Then we can press through to God's consolation, even without demanding an answer to our question. So many of God's great followers – Moses, David, Jeremiah – all knew the hurt of thorns. I can identify with these, and feel part of their stories. Indeed, I can now thank God for the pressure of his hands in forming my 'jar of clay'. Certainly I agree that, in coming to terms with our individual thorns, 'in acceptance lies peace'. As we travel down the dark tunnel caused by a thorn, we need the full radiance of God's glory in the face of Jesus Christ, to transform us into 'more than conquerors'. As we accept the privilege of being transformed by the hands of God into the image of his Son – which is, at least, part of the reason for the suffering – we may not experience the removal of the thorn, or an understanding of the thorn, but we may arrive at an acceptance of God's grace in sending us our thorn – and, in fact, even come to say: 'Thank you, God, for entrusting me with this thorn, even if you never tell me why!'

Helen Roseveare, retired missionary doctor

One of the greatest challenges for Christians, in their thinking and feeling both for themselves and for others, is how to deal with the problem of pain. Here Pablo Martinez works at it helpfully from his different positions as believer, psychiatrist and long-term sufferer threatened with blindness. This book, which is wholly biblically based, is very clearly, and at times humorously, written. I would wholeheartedly recommend it as a 'descendant' of C. S. Lewis' *The Problem of Pain*, brought into the twenty-first century. From his own perspective, working over many years with his own suffering, and from his deep knowledge and understanding of the Bible, especially biblical characters, Pablo has written from what he has observed and used in helping patients. His chapter on 'Acceptance' is supremely practical, and the author is never satisfied with a lather of simple-minded positive thinking. He is devastatingly clear-sighted and penetrating in his insights. Although he is writing primarily for Christians, anyone undergoing or witnessing suffering would find this book strengthening. I shall have no hesitation in sending it to friends who are struggling with pain, whether they are believers or not. This is a valuable new contribution from one who has greatly aided the church in his previous writings.

Andrew Sims, Emeritus Professor of Psychiatry, University of Leeds;
Past President, Royal College of Psychiatrists

PABLO MARTINEZ

A THORN in the Flesh

FINDING STRENGTH AND HOPE AMID SUFFERING

ivp

INTER-VARSITY PRESS
Norton Street, Nottingham NG7 3HR, England
Email: ivp@ivpbooks.com
Website: www.ivpbooks.com

First published 2007

British Library Cataloguing in Publication Data
A catalogue record for this book is available from the British Library.

ISBN 978-1-84474-188-5

Set in 10.5/13pt Dante
Typeset in Great Britain by CRB Associates, Reepham, Norfolk
Printed and bound in Great Britain by Ashford Colour Press Ltd, Gosport,
Hampshire

Inter-Varsity Press publishes Christian books that are true to the Bible and that
communicate the gospel, develop discipleship and strengthen the church for its
mission in the world.

Inter-Varsity Press is closely linked with the Universities and Colleges Christian
Fellowship, a student movement connecting Christian Unions in universities and
colleges throughout Great Britain, and a member movement of the International
Fellowship of Evangelical Students. Website: www.uccf.org.uk

Contents

Acknowledgments

Several key people made this book possible. I would like to express my gratitude, first of all, to James and Joyce Phillips, who spent many hours translating the major part of the manuscript into English. My sincere thanks also go to those who arranged the personal testimonies or helped with the English version: Debbie Vila, Roger Marshall, Jonathan Dawson and Birthe Munck-Fairwood.

I owe many thanks to those who read through the manuscript and made very helpful comments. Among them, I am very much indebted to my father, whose pastoral heart and theological expertise provided me with invaluable suggestions. I should also make a special mention of Eleanor Trotter, who had the vision for this book and asked me to write it. From the very beginning she was determined to make this work as a source of help and hope.

I am greatly indebted to the individuals who were willing to open up their hearts and share the pain of their own life stories. Their personal testimonies at the end of the book are a vivid example of how God can provide strength and comfort in the midst of trials, and I deeply appreciate the time and effort they took to write them.

Finally, a heartfelt word of gratitude to my loved ones – my wife, Marta, my parents and my sisters Elisabeth and Ana – whose support and closeness have been decisive in helping me through the rough times with my thorn.

Pablo Martinez

Foreword

From the very first paragraph of the introduction to this book, I could identify with its purpose – to provide strength and hope, through responding to some of life's toughest questions.

I am sure most of us have been asked many times, 'If there *is* a God of love, why is there so much suffering in the world?' Pablo Martinez, with his personal experience of 'thorns', does not give glib answers but provides a well-balanced, well-researched and biblical commentary on suffering of all kinds.

He deals in detail with the thorns Paul endured throughout his life as a follower of Christ, and explains these thorns as loss – whether of health, limb, freedom or a loved one – and explores the resultant emotions, such as anger, depression and anxiety. He illustrates all this with stories of characters from the Bible, such as Job, Jacob and David.

The necessity, he says, is to deal with these emotions rather than continuing to nurture them, which often results in strained and even broken relationships with family and loved ones. It has been said that to begin to understand someone's suffering we have to walk a mile in their shoes, thus avoiding giving a trite biblical sermon, which can be at the very least irritating! What people are looking for initially is affirmation, not explanation.

In his *Journals*, the Danish philosopher Søren Kierkegaard said. 'Life can only be understood backwards, but it has to be lived forwards.' How true! So often, when we look back on the tough times of our lives, we realize how much we have learned through them. I learnt, when I became a Christian, that it's not so much *what* happens to us but how we *handle* what happens to us that's important. This can be done only by trusting God, even when we don't understand.

Pablo Martinez says that 'the way in which we face our own thorns in life is the best "sermon" that we can ever preach', and the book concludes with some very moving testimonies, which illustrate this point beautifully.

I am sure *A Thorn in the Flesh* will prove to be a very useful resource for those suffering from their own thorns as well as for those aiming to give help and comfort.

Fiona Castle
June 2007

Introduction

'We have lost our health but not our joy; we have lost our hair but not our smile; they can take our life away but not our hope.' These words, serene yet firm, were spoken to me by a woman whose husband had been battling cancer for several years. Her face reflected extreme tiredness, but not bitterness; pain, but not gloom. She was injured by a thorn, but not defeated. As she spoke to me I thought, 'How can this afflicted woman fight and accept at the same time? Does she know some "secret" that enables her to face *chronic* suffering – in its multiple manifestations – with dignity and fortitude?' Suddenly, an idea crossed my mind: the way in which we face our own thorns in life is the best 'sermon' that we can ever preach. Is it not true that the way Jesus lived with the thorn of the cross – from Gethsemane until the moment he died – is the most extraordinary moral rubric of his exemplary life?

The words and attitude of the woman just mentioned perfectly summarize the purpose of this book: to focus on the light of hope rather than on the darkness of the trial; to speak of victory rather than defeat; not to be paralysed by the thorn's venom but rather to be strengthened by the supernatural antidote of grace. In synthesis, this is a book not primarily about suffering but about the power of Christ, which makes us 'more than conquerors' in the face of any trial. We must be careful, however, not to become confused: there is no room for triumphalism. To be more than conquerors does not mean that we have magical formulae that eliminate thorns or their pain, as in a fairy tale. Victory is forged along a costly road that ultimately leads to serene acceptance and experiencing the power of Christ that is perfected in our weakness. As we travel down this path, we are transformed emotionally and spiritually. We will not be the same again when we discover that a tragedy can also be an opportunity, that we can be victims or heroes depending on how we respond to crisis, that the darkest night is also dotted with stars.

The book is intended to provide strength and hope by responding to very practical questions. As we mention these questions, we also anticipate some of its key ideas:

- What was the secret that enabled Paul to transform a weakness into a gift? We will learn how the thorn constantly reminded him not so much of his *inadequacy*, but of Christ's full *adequacy*.
- What is acceptance, and what is it not? How can we achieve a mature and biblical view of this 'key weapon' that enables us to see the thorn with different eyes and think of it positively? To accept means reaching the serene conviction that God can use my life not only *in spite of* my thorn, but *through* it.
- What is the practical role of grace in helping us overcome the thorn? Grace moulds our natural reactions, such as anger, anxiety, low self-esteem and depression. But, above all, grace is the sum of supernatural resources that enables us to battle with divine power.
- Can we do something to recover the meaning of life and avoid bitterness? What is 'happiness' for a Christian? Grace changes our view not only of the thorn, but of the whole of life. Paul learnt not only acceptance, but a completely new set of priorities.

Let me close this introduction by sharing a personal word, which I hope will help the reader to feel closer to the author. I am not writing from the distant, comfortable and disinterested position of the person who has hardly been touched by suffering. I have struggled almost all my life against a tough thorn. An eye disease, juvenile glaucoma, has been 'buffeting' me since I was eighteen years old. I have suffered the stressful experience of eye surgery twelve times. Visual impairment, with all its consequences, is my undesired 'companion'. Even today, as I am finishing this book, another bout of surgery seems inevitable. The thorn is still here. However, when I look over my life as a whole, from its very beginning, I can clearly discern God's faithfulness guiding and providing. I have experienced that the Lord is my Shepherd always, but especially when I am walking through the shadowy valleys of life, because his shadow, the Shadow of the Almighty, is my keeper.

In Christ, my weakness is his strength. For this reason I firmly trust the promise in James 1:12:

> Blessed is the man who perseveres under trial, because when he has stood [endured] the test, he will receive the crown of life that God has promised to those who love him.

This is my heartfelt desire and prayer for the readers of this book.

Pablo Martinez
June 2007

1 Paul's thorn and ours: identifying the enemy

. . . there was given me a thorn in my flesh, a messenger of Satan, to torment me (2 Corinthians 12:7).

If you carefully turn your eyes back
To your life, you will understand
Things which you could not understand earlier,
In as much as, after patiently gazing at the sky,
You get to discover one by one, thousands of stars
Where hitherto only darkness could be seen.[1]

The uncontained excitement of young parents over their first child is suddenly extinguished when he is born with severe cerebral palsy. A thirty-year-old mother has to forsake her profession as a teacher, only recently commenced after many years of preparation, due to a degenerative disease of the retina. A forty-five-year-old man tries to find new meaning for his life after a senseless traffic accident leaves him in a wheelchair. He struggles against being eaten up by bitterness and resentment; it is hard for him to forgive the drunk driver who destroyed his life for ever. The parents of a drug addict suffering from a personality disorder are deeply distressed and heartbroken because of the problems their son recurrently creates, causing them to live in a bottomless pit of pain.

These are real people whom I have met and tried to help in the last few years. All of them – and their families – have something in common: they once felt powerless, defeated, perplexed and weak in the face of traumas that unexpectedly shook their lives. They all struggled hard for a long time in an attempt to overcome and accept their thorns: situations of lengthy – maybe endless – periods of suffering, whether due to illness, disabilities, serious family or relationship problems, or even persecution for their faith with all its consequences: exile, poverty, rejection, discrimination. Their journey through the 'dark night of crisis' was long, even tortuous sometimes. Step by step, however, they were able to find light as well as hope. Following their life stories has been a most inspiring and challenging experience.

What is a thorn?

We must first define the terrain, because the subject of suffering is very broad. When we speak of a thorn, what kind of trial do we have in mind? The definition I use here is not exclusive. There can be different approaches, all of them very enriching. My definition of 'thorn' has been guided by two basic patterns: on the one hand, Paul's first-hand knowledge as described in 2 Corinthians 12:7–10. A detailed and progressive analysis of this fertile passage will be the backbone of this book. The apostle's experience expressed in Scripture gives us the basis needed to approach the subject *objectively*. However, I want to include a *subjective* element: my own suffering for more than twenty-five years, coupled with that of many of my patients, whose life journeys, shared in the intimacy of my doctor's office, have enriched my understanding of the problem extraordinarily. By combining these two approaches, a thorn can be defined as a situation of **chronic suffering** in which we find five distinctive traits:

- It is **painful**. It makes you feel **broken** inside. Whether the pain is physical, or, even worse, emotional and moral, the thorn is very painful. *'The soul's pain is worse than the body's pain.'* It is deep, and sometimes agonizing and heartbreaking.

- It is **limiting**. It causes you to feel **helpless**. It reduces your autonomy, your worth and even your personal freedom. Because the thorn affects your physical mobility or independence, it nearly always imposes *limitations*. You have to stop doing things that you could previously do. The thorn implies the loss and relinquishment of many things.
- It is **humiliating**. It makes you feel weak and small. It produces a deep alteration in self-esteem because of its own consequences: physical, emotional or social. Physical appearance, job or personal relationships can end up being greatly affected by the thorn, with feelings of inferiority and identity crises. 'Who am I now?' Weakness is a constant characteristic.
- It is **prolonged**. The painful situation does not improve with time – it can last for years, sometimes a lifetime. It can be constant or repetitive, showing up in recurring episodes. Partial relief can be found, but the basic problem persists. A sharp and brief pain does not fit into the category of a thorn.
- It implies **battle**. It is a battle with oneself, with circumstances and with God. One fights to change what can be changed and to accept the unchangeable. It is a fight that leads to defeating adversity, rather than letting oneself be defeated by adversity. It is a struggle that makes you depend more every day on the grace of Jesus Christ, on his strength and on his comfort.

Some examples of thorns

Within this framework, there are many possible thorn situations. At the end of the book you will find an appendix with a more detailed list that may help you identify your own thorn. Here I will just refer to the main types. You may add your own or indeed any form of chronic recurrent suffering.

A thorn may stem from:

Chronic physical or psychiatric illnesses

On many occasions these are degenerative, incapacitating and recurring at the same time. **Cancer**, in its multiple forms, is a very special thorn. Only a few years ago we would not have included it here because unfortunately it would have been considered an acute and not a chronic process. Today, however, a high percentage of cancer patients have become chronic patients, surviving with the disease for many years.[2]

Some *emotional disturbances* are not illnesses per se but rather specific traits of personality or temperament. The person suffers and struggles to get rid of these traits which have become a problem to them. Some examples are identity conflicts, feelings of inferiority or of just being *different*, extreme shyness or an explosive personality where there is difficulty in exerting self-control.

Disabilities
These can be physical or psychological in nature. Sometimes they result from accidents or illnesses, for example different degrees of paralysis, affecting part of the body (hemiplegia), or even the four extremities (tetraplegia). At other times the disabilities stem from birth: infant cerebral palsy, Down's syndrome or genetic diseases.

Serious relational conflicts
These can occur within the family (with children, among siblings, between spouses), in the church or between friends. Throughout this book we will see how some relationship problems have all the characteristics of being a thorn. We have the clearest example in David in the Old Testament, persecuted by Saul for many years. Later on the thorn arose from within his own family, the drama of being harassed by his son Absalom lasting several years.

Persecution due to one's faith
You may be surprised to find this type of thorn included here. It is, however, a reality: some thorns are the direct result of complete obedience to our Lord. Such was the reality for the believers in the church at Smyrna, the only church other than the one at Philadelphia that was not rebuked (Revelation 2:8–11). Their material poverty was quite probably the consequence of their faith and valiant testimony. As a result, they had suffered pillage, the spoiling of their belongings, loss of jobs, and persistent harassment, mainly at the hands of the Jews living in the city. They had lost everything, 'yet you are rich' (v. 9), the angel told them; 'Do not be afraid of what you are about to suffer.' On other occasions, the consequences of suffering for our faith are more subtle, but no less painful: undesired loneliness, for example, as in the experience of Jeremiah.

Today, more than ever before, thousands of people around the world suffer the dramatic consequences of faithfully following Jesus Christ in a society that rejects God.[3] The thorns that these modern-day martyrs suffer because of their faith deserve an entire book![4] Discrimination, poverty, scorn, imprisonment and physical torture are the daily accompaniments of faith for many Christians today. May these lines be a humble recognition and a heartfelt tribute to our extended family in the persecuted church. We pray fervently for them, asking God to strengthen them in the midst of the thorns they suffer through persecution.

The whole family suffers

It is important to notice that, almost always, the thorn affects the whole family. Sometimes it is even harder for the family than for the person suffering directly from it. This is particularly true in certain cases of deficiency and mental disorder where the awareness of the situation on the part of the person affected is low or even nil. In such instances, the pain, the feelings of helplessness or the desire to fight do not appear in the one suffering so much as in their family. It is similar when the thorn is the result of the behaviour or attitudes of another person close to us. For example, in alcoholism, drug addiction, compulsive gambling or other such problems, the fallout is often much greater among the family members than for the person affected, who may not even see that there is a problem.

Paul's thorn

I will seek to answer three questions about Paul's thorn:

- Its nature: what were its characteristics?
- Its interpretation: what did it mean?
- Its origin: where did it come from?

Its nature: What were its characteristics?

What do we know of Paul's affliction? As we explore the meaning of the word 'thorn', we understand some of its essential traits. The word used here, *skolops*, originally denoted anything sharp, such as a pointed stake. Fitted with a metal point, it was used to prod along oxen and cavalry horses. In classical Greek it could also refer to the stake used to impale certain criminals. Nonetheless, it also came to mean 'thorn' and was thus used in the Old Testament (cf. Numbers 33:55; Ezekiel 28:24; Hosea 2:6).

We cannot be certain what this *skolops* might have been in Paul's life. However, the text (2 Corinthians 12) clearly describes certain aspects that help us understand its nature. Even though we do not know with absolute certainty *what* it was, we have enough light to know *how* it affected the apostle. For example, we know that it was a **humiliating** experience: it *'torments me'* (v. 7). Paul felt not only injured but also humiliated. Somehow the thorn affected his self-esteem, because he felt outraged. We can also deduce that it was a recurring, **repetitive**, suffering – probably in the form of crises or episodes – 'three times I pleaded with the Lord to take it away from me' (v. 8) – and apparently the thorn accompanied him throughout his life. We will explore these two aspects in greater detail in the next chapter, when we consider Paul's reactions.

From the metaphor used, we deduce that it was also **painful**. The word used indicates a very intense pain, almost unbearable, probably physical in nature. Lightfoot describes it as 'a stake plunged through the flesh'. And, in Calvin's words, the intensity of the pain is deduced, 'for if it had been slight, or easy to be endured, he would not have been so desirous to be freed from it'.[5] What is emphasized, however, by the metaphor is the intensity of the suffering and its effects. Therefore, in Paul's thorn we find the traits mentioned earlier.

Interpretation of the thorn: what was it?

What was Paul's thorn? How are we to interpret this metaphor? Countless answers have been given, something which indicates in itself the difficulty of reaching a definite conclusion. It is probably best looked at this way. It must not have been by chance that the Holy Spirit, when inspiring the text of 2 Corinthians 12, permitted a certain level of ambiguity, which in turn gives us the freedom to think about our own thorns. Thus, each of us can identify with Paul's situation. More than likely there is some truth in the different interpretations that have been made throughout history, some by reputed commentators such as Calvin or Luther. This allows us to think that, even though in a strict sense there was only one thorn, Paul suffered from a number of problems that fall within the range of characteristics we have described.

- **Spiritual temptation.** Some identify the thorn with a spiritual problem, specifically the temptations that Paul undoubtedly faced from the devil. 'The temptation to doubt, to shirk the duties of the apostolic life, the sting of conscience when these temptations conquered.'[6] This was Calvin's view. This seems, however, to be an excessively vague and generic interpretation, taking into account that Paul alludes to a very specific fact with particular characteristics that differ greatly from a problem as broad in scope as spiritual temptation.
- **Opposition and persecution.** Others think that the thorn refers to the numerous persecutions Paul suffered from both the Jews and the Roman authorities. He goes as far as describing them in detail in his epistles. He likewise suffered opposition within the church, sometimes from specific people, and this apparently affected him seriously. Examples of this are 'Alexander the metalworker, who did me a great deal of harm' (2 Timothy 4:14), and Hymenaeus and Philetus (2 Timothy 2:17). This was Luther's interpretation. However, this clashes with the reality that Paul never prayed to be freed from persecution. Rather, he accepted (assumed) it to be something to be expected in the Christian life. As he told Timothy, 'everyone who wants to live a godly life in Christ Jesus will be persecuted' (2 Timothy 3:12).
- **Carnal temptation.** In the Middle Ages the thorn was interpreted (particularly among monks) as carnal temptation, perhaps as a result of the sexual restrictions particular to monasticism. The thorn was an instrument for mortifying the flesh in order to combat the tendency to lascivious thoughts. This is the position held by the Roman Catholic Church. The problem with this exegesis is that it contradicts Paul's words in 1 Corinthians 7:7–9, where he gives us to understand that God has given him the gift of abstinence.
- **His physical appearance.** It has been suggested that Paul could have suffered from some type of physical malformation, possibly of his face, giving him an unpleasant appearance at first sight which might have been an obstacle in his work. 'According to a

second-century tradition he was unattractive, small, even ugly, with a bald head, beetle brows, bandy legs and a hooked nose.'[7] The remark made by the Corinthians would go along with this line: 'His bodily presence is weak and his speech contemptible' (2 Corinthians 10:10, NKJV). Of course, this is nothing like the leaders that the world idolizes today, with their handsomely appealing image. Paul would probably have failed as a twenty-first-century communicator.

- **A physical illness.** Some people maintain that his thorn was an infectious disease contracted on one of his missionary journeys and that it caused recurring episodes of high fever, a symptom of **malaria**, or some other infectious disease, such as **brucellosis**. And a good number of people suggest some form of **epilepsy**, which would fit in well with the repetitive nature of the crises and the periods in which he was free of symptoms and during which he could carry on a normal life. Others suggest **migraine** crises, severe headaches causing him to be bedridden for several days at a time. In fact, these crises are all compatible with the previous interpretations, since high fevers as well as certain forms of epilepsy can be accompanied by intense headaches. This opinion was maintained by some church fathers, such as Jerome.

- **A problem with his eyes.** A number of indications point in this direction. In Galatians 4:15 Paul writes, '... if you could have done so, you would have torn out your eyes and given them to me'. And at the end of this same epistle he writes, in 6:11, 'See what large letters I use as I write to you with my own hand!' His writing leads us to think he had very reduced sharpness of vision. Another passage that indicates a similar possibility is Acts 23:1–5. When Paul was before the Council and called Ananias a 'whitewashed wall', he was reprimanded by others, who said to him, 'You dare to insult God's high priest?' (v. 4). To this Paul replied, 'Brothers, I did not realize that he was the high priest' (v. 5), which alludes to a probable visual impairment. Undoubtedly, Paul would have correctly identified the high priest had his vision been first-rate.

These eye problems might have been the result of the experience he had on the Damascus road, when a light flashed from heaven, leaving him blind for three days (Acts 9:3–9). According to some experts, Paul's retinas could have suffered considerable damage, from which they never fully recovered. The problems might also have been due to something affecting his corneas, which would explain the recurring and painful nature of his crises.[8] Many commentators, seeing in Paul's weak eyes the best indication that he depended completely on God's grace, hold this position.

Which of these interpretations is correct? Even if we accept that all of them might contain some truth, in my opinion Paul's thorn was physical. I am therefore inclined to think that the most accurate interpretation is to be found among the last three options. This idea is reinforced by Paul's own testimony when he explicitly alludes to its being 'a trial to you in my bodily condition' (Galatians 4:14, NASB). 'And that which was a trial to you in my bodily condition you did not despise or loathe, but you received me as an angel of God, as Christ Jesus Himself.' This is the opinion held by F. F. Bruce: 'It was probably the bodily ailment which he suffered when he first visited the Galatians – an ailment which was a *trial* to them as well as to him and which might have been expected to repel them or make them spit in aversion.'[9]

Even though we cannot dismiss the possibility of epilepsy and malaria, which are plausible hypotheses, my personal inclinations lead me to believe that Paul's thorn was his eyesight problem. I must confess that my reasons are partly due to personal identification, suffering as I have from my own thorn in my eyes since I was eighteen.

The origin of the thorn: punishment from God or 'a messenger of Satan'?

Why me? What have I done for this to happen to me? This is one of the first questions we ask when a thorn enters our life. And the answer must also be clear from the outset: the trial does not come from God but from Satan. Paul knew this very well and therefore does not hesitate for one instant to identify the origin of his trial: 'a messenger of Satan'. It is Satan, and not God, who takes the initiative in the realm of tribulation. In an exceptional way, to be sure, God can send a trial with the intention of setting an example. The clearest case is that of Ananias and Sapphira (Acts 5:1–11), whose death served as an example of correction for the young church in Jerusalem. There are very few occasions when the Bible points out a clear relationship between sin and trial, as in the case of King David's family tragedy, which was the result of his own sin (see 2 Samuel 12:10–12). But this is the exception rather than the rule. It is Satan who is behind suffering, not God.

This principle is stated very clearly in the case of Job (Job 1:7–11). In the New Testament, the apostle James also expresses it clearly: 'When tempted, no-one should say, God is tempting me. For God cannot be tempted by evil, nor does he tempt anyone' (James 1:13). Peter expresses the same idea, using a simile: 'the devil prowls around like a roaring lion looking for someone to devour' (1 Peter 5:8).

We cannot, however, become extremists, seeing the devil everywhere we look. This view, popular in some circles, sees specific demons as being the cause of every trial and tribulation. More prominence is given to Satan than to Christ. I know of so-called Christian books on the subject in which the names of God or Jesus are hardly mentioned. Maybe it is not deliberate, but it must be considered an error with serious consequences. In order to correct this error, we must look at certain practical aspects of suffering in the light of biblical teaching, responding to the questions that people have asked so frequently over many years.

'Who sinned, this man or his parents?'

Has this come upon me because of some sin that I have committed? This question torments many believers. Attributing a cause-and-effect relationship between the thorn and divine punishment is well rooted in the human mind, being a characteristic of many religions and even of paganism. This was how Job's friends thought. But it is such a mistaken idea that it even stirred God's anger against such unhelpful comforters (see Job 42:7). This was also what the people who approached Jesus thought: 'Who sinned, this man or his parents, that he was born blind?' The Lord's answer is as forceful as it is comforting: 'Neither this man nor his parents sinned, but this happened so that the work of God might be displayed in his life' (John 9:2–3). Jesus emphasizes this principle in Luke 13:1–5 with two other examples. On this occasion, Jesus asks the question: 'Do you think that these Galileans were worse sinners … because they suffered this way?' In both cases Jesus answers with a forceful 'I tell you, no!' 'Truncheon theology' presupposes a practical negation of divine grace in that it devalues Christ's sacrifice. If my suffering is a way to pay for my sins and guilt, where then is the merit of the blood of Christ?

Problem or gift? 'There was given me . . .'

Paul knew this 'lesson' very well! One of the most striking aspects of the passage is the way in which the apostle refers to the thorn. He does not say, 'I was punished with' nor even 'the Lord permitted'. The verb 'to give' in the original Greek, *didōmi*, has an unequivocal positive connotation, as if it were a gift. It could also be translated 'there was granted me'. The apostle lived that experience, not as a punishment but as a favour or special grace. In God's hands, the thorn ceased to be a curse and became a source of blessing. What was Paul's secret, which enabled him to transform a problem into a gift? At this point it is enough to anticipate this idea: the thorn constantly reminded him not so much of his *inadequacy*, but of Christ's full *adequacy* to strengthen him. Herein lies the essence of accepting our thorns, and the central argument of this book.

There are many sins without disease (thorns), and many diseases without sin. If God had to punish us with a thorn for every sin we committed, the world would be a gigantic hospital. No, God does not treat us as we deserve but according to the 'manifold grace' of Christ that 'purifies us from all sin' (1 Peter 4:10; 1 John 1:7).

Not because of my sins but because of sin

If it is clear that there is no specific sin behind the majority of thorns, then what is their origin? Of course, there is no explanation for each particular case. We have already seen how Jesus categorically disqualifies any attempt to argue in favour of this. We must therefore ask the broader question: where does evil come from? Why is there so much suffering in the world? This is not the place for an exhaustive analysis. A person suffering from a thorn does not so much need the depth of clever arguments as they do the warmth of a hand or the comforting gaze of a loving face.

Nevertheless, there is one basic idea that we need to understand: thorns enter our lives because we live in an abnormal world, one that is dislocated by sin.

What is sin and how did it all begin? The story is not complicated and can be explained using the simile of marriage. Just as happens with many couples today, man and woman did not want to live 'bound' to God, in a relationship of permanent love and mutual commitment. They wanted to be free and independent. As a result they used the option of separation that God had previously given them. A love relationship is always voluntary – no one can ever be retained by force because it is then no longer a love relationship but kidnapping.

By making use of the option of separation, man and woman became estranged from God. But, just as happens in divorce, such a decision comes with natural consequences that are implicit in the fracture of the relationship. Like the collapse of a house of cards, the rupture with their Creator swept other relationships along with it. From that moment on, man and woman entered a *state*, an existential situation of profound dislocation that we call 'sin'. The Greek term, *hamartia*, alludes to something that has lost its original structure. It is dislocated or fractured. The Bible describes it by saying, 'the whole creation has been groaning as in the pains of childbirth right up to the present time. Not only so, but we ourselves, who have the firstfruits of the Spirit, groan inwardly as we wait eagerly for our adoption as sons, the redemption of our bodies' (Romans 8:22–23).

This is how suffering appeared in all of its facets: on the one hand, the pain caused by humans to each other – war, murder, violence, the exploitation of the weakest and the fracture in the social arena. The damage that emanates from nature then appeared: diseases, natural catastrophes, and the great tragedies in which humanity is not so much the offender as the victim. And then there was that inner restlessness or disquiet, that personal emptiness so well described by atheist existentialists, which led Sartre to exclaim, 'The Nausea has not left me, it is I.'[10]

God allows, but sets limits: 'the devil's passport'

We have seen two important principles: a thorn does not come from God, nor is it punishment for a specific sin, and suffering is linked with Satan. We need to understand a third and final idea: God allows thorns. The Satanic antagonism that cruelly oppressed Job, Paul's thorn, and all other trials, are known and allowed by God, a statement I will clarify in a way that will help us to understand it better.

God sets limits on a trial; both suffering and Satan are under his control. Satan does not have free rein to oppress and besiege as he fancies. First, he must have God's permission, a principle understood from Jesus' words, 'Satan *has asked* to sift you as wheat' (Luke 22:31). We also see this principle clearly in Job, when God sets specific boundaries that Satan cannot go beyond: 'Everything he has is in your hands, but on the man himself do not lay a finger' (Job 1:12). The apostle Paul expresses it with great strength and clarity in one of his most comforting and lucid texts on this subject, 'God is faithful: He will not let you be tried *beyond* what you are able to bear, but with the trial will also provide a way out so that you may be able to endure it' (1 Corinthians 10:13, NETB). God permits trials and tests, but there is a limit, a boundary, established by him, which Satan cannot overstep. We could say that Satan 'travels' with a passport containing visas supplied by God; Satan cannot enter a country – touch a person – without the approval of the Almighty.

In the case of Job, the limit was his life: Satan could not kill him. However, we have no guarantee that it will always be that way. The same God who freed Peter from prison almost at the same time allowed James the brother of John to be beheaded (Acts 12:2). This reminds us of the value of human life: for the believer in Jesus Christ, physical life is not an absolute value, nor what is most important. We must be careful when making an affirmation like this in an age in which the value of life is relative and despised by so many, from the defenders of euthanasia to terrorists. I believe without reservation in the sanctity of life, in its sacred quality that makes every human being unique. But there is something above physical life, and that is spiritual life: the soul. If living is important, living eternally is vital. The Lord Jesus himself taught us, 'Do not be afraid of those who kill the body but cannot kill the soul. Rather, be afraid of the one who can destroy both soul and body in hell' (Matthew 10:28).

All this opens up a different perspective on the concept of health that goes far beyond the absence of illness or being in good physical shape – there is a very important spiritual dimension.

Even though it is sometimes difficult to understand and believe, God controls the general course of history and my life in particular. It is this way because God's providence, mysterious as it may seem, is above the limited power of the evil one.

Christ is stronger than Satan

Our Lord defeated Satan on the cross. Christ has much greater power than the evil one, from whom we have nothing to fear. Christ is conqueror and the strength of the early church based on the *Christus victor* is the same today. We must, therefore, not overvalue Satan's ability. But neither should we minimize it. C. S. Lewis used to say that the devil is overjoyed with either of these two extremes: the denial of his existence or living obsessed with him.

Satan's power is real but limited; he is under the control of 'the God of peace [who] will soon crush Satan under your feet' (Romans 16:20). Shortly before his death, Jesus said, 'In the world you will have tribulation. But take heart; I have overcome the world' (John 16:33, ESV). If you still have any doubts about this, read the book of Revelation, a book as difficult to interpret as its central message is simple: **Jesus Christ overcomes**. Even in the midst of the scourge of a thorn, the believer can exclaim, with absolute certainty, 'Satan can oppress me but he cannot destroy me.' Make the beautiful words of the hymn 'We rest on thee' your own:

> We rest on Thee, our Shield and our Defender!
> We go not forth alone against the foe;
> Strong in Thy strength, safe in Thy keeping tender,
> We rest on Thee, and in Thy Name we go.
>
> We go in faith, our own great weakness feeling,
> And needing more each day Thy grace to know:
> Yet from our hearts a song of triumph pealing,
> 'We rest on Thee, and in Thy Name we go.'

The last verse ends in a firm declaration of victory in Christ:

> When passing through the gates of pearly splendour,
> *Victors*, we rest with Thee, through endless days.

God and human suffering: brief practical considerations

God's action in suffering contains mystery and consolation. In fact, it contains much more comfort than mystery. Continuing with the simile of Albert Schweitzer quoted at the beginning of the chapter, it is like a window that opens onto a night scene: I can focus more on the darkness or on the stars, on the heartbreaking blow of the tribulation or on the balm of divine comfort. The purpose of this book is to help you to fix your gaze more on the 'stars' and discover the healing aspects of God's providence in the midst of the storms of life. This will make the road to acceptance easier to travel, enabling us to learn to live *with* and not *in opposition to* the thorn.

This is not a book on the *theory* of suffering but on dealing with the thorn in a *practical* way. We will therefore deliberately not spend time on the complicated philosophical or theological reasoning behind the origin of evil, which has already been covered in other books.[11] Having said this, though, there are some considerations that are essential here because of their practical implications. Each one seeks to respond, albeit briefly, to four questions frequently asked by the person who suffers:

- Why?
- How can I understand it?
- Where is God?
- What is God doing?

God has the 'right' to keep secrets: the value of mystery

'Why?' This is usually the first question a person asks when going through a rough time. Many people have become estranged from God at this point because they did not find the answers they expected. Their faith was shipwrecked in the face of God's apparent silence: 'I stopped believing when my forty-year-old brother died, leaving behind a widow and three young children'; 'Unanswered questions accumulated in my mind until I realized that I no longer felt I was a believer'; 'A God that does nothing about suffering is a God that is of no value to me.' How do we respond?

This is a subject in which we do not have the answer to every question. Our knowledge will always be incomplete. There are elements of mystery that belong to 'God's secrets'. Why so? If God were not involved in 'glorious enigmas', as Joni Eareckson Tada calls them,[12] he would somehow cease to be God. This is expressed clearly in Scripture: 'The secret things belong to the LORD our God, but the things revealed belong to us and to our children for ever . . .' (Deuteronomy 29:29). Or, 'Can you fathom the mysteries of God?' (Job 11:7). We therefore have to accept that the Almighty 'hides' certain realities from us. The word *mystērion* in fact means 'veiled', 'hidden'. Faith would lose a major part of its very essence, and attraction, if we knew everything. So mystery is of essential value to faith. God, in his sovereignty, has chosen to reveal many things to us, but he has also chosen to keep other things hidden. As the French thinker Paul Claudel once said: 'Jesus did not come to explain suffering, but in order to fill it with His presence.'

It can be useful for us to remember the story of Jacob when he lost his dear son Joseph. God spoke directly to him on seven different occasions, always at key points in his life. The messages from God said that Jacob had been chosen by God, that God was with him and that he was not to worry – all messages of great reassurance. One day, Jacob's sons arrived home with the blood-soaked tunic of his favourite son, and they told their father he had died. God knew the truth, he loved Jacob and he saw his affliction, yet he didn't say anything. Jacob must have cried out to God, asking, 'Why?' 'What about all those dreams and the promises you gave me?' But God was preparing something that would protect and preserve Jacob and his family in the future. If Jacob had known at that point that his son was alive, he would have set out to rescue him. This would have ruined God's plan. So, despite the pain, God kept silent on this matter for about twenty years. The silence was broken only when Jacob was told that Joseph was alive, and then he set out for Egypt, where his family was preserved from famine.

These hidden treasures encourage our search for truth and, as a result, our dependence upon God. This is what Solomon thought: 'It is the glory of God to conceal a matter; to search out a matter is the glory of kings' (Proverbs 25:2). In Joni's own words, 'It is God's nature to hide things. I discovered that early on in my life with Christ. Somehow I knew if I desired a deeper, more intimate knowledge of the Lord, I would be sent on a search. There were treasures to dig. Precious gems to mine.'[13] We shall never have all the answers, but we do have sufficient answers to face the challenge of a thorn with faith. Our understanding of the matter is incomplete, but not unsatisfactory. This takes us to the second question.

The light is found only in the light: faith as a starting point

'How can I understand it?' Suffering is a road filled with twists and bends, with shadows and darkness, but also with rays of shining bright light that help us see beyond the apparent reality of our present pain. It is like a surrealist painting: it always leaves windows open to mystery, windows through which faith enters. These twists and bends with shadows disappear only in God's presence, when his light dissipates the darkness. It is impossible to find light in darkness. The answers to the subject of suffering, even though they are partial, will not be found in introspection or in philosophy, but in him who said of himself, 'I am the light of the world' (John 8:12). Herein lies the full reality of the Psalmist's saying, 'in your light we see light' (Psalm 36:9b). This will happen in an absolute and perfect way when we are in God's presence, as Isaiah beautifully describes: 'Your sun will never set again, and your moon will wane no more; the LORD will be your everlasting light, and your days of sorrow will end' (Isaiah 60:20). But, even now, in an incomplete way, rays of light penetrate, helping us to understand key aspects of this subject.

Faith, therefore, however how simple it may be, is an essential prerequisite to understanding the mysteries of suffering. We are not referring to 'gap-filling faith', a faith opposed to reason, which has been a stumbling block to many, especially to young people. We are referring more to the faith of Blaise Pascal, to whom is attributed the statement, 'The heart has reasons that reason does not understand.'

God suffers with us: my tears are his tears

'Where is God when I am suffering so much?' This is one of the most frequent and logical questions from the fiery furnace. God seems distant and silent. But his distance and silence are only apparent. God is there – right there – because he cries with and in us. There is ample evidence in the Bible to affirm that not only did God suffer in Christ but he continues to suffer with his people today. In my suffering, God is not impassive, like stone, but sensitive like a seismograph. The slightest sigh, the weakest groan, is registered in his heart. No tear that runs down my cheek is unknown to God, who has said, 'In all their distress he too was distressed' (Isaiah 63:9), or in his emotive words through the prophet Hosea, 'How can I give you up? . . . My heart is changed within me; all my compassion is aroused' (Hosea 11:8). It is difficult to find a more intense expression of sympathy, understanding and identification.

God knows my suffering, not only in the cognitive sense, of being *informed*, but also in the experiential sense: he *experiences* my suffering with me. 'I have surely seen the affliction of my people . . . and have heard their cry because of their taskmasters. I know their sufferings' (Exodus 3:7, ESV). We must remember that the Hebrew word for 'know' implies a great intimacy. The idea that God does not suffer – the doctrine of impassiveness – has no biblical basis. The very essence of God's character, that he is love, rejects such a notion. This is logical. If God were incapable of suffering, he would also be incapable of loving. He who does not weep, loves not; he who loves, weeps. 'What meaning can there be in a love which is not costly to the lover?'[14]

As someone has said, 'an impassive God would be an infinite iceberg of metaphysics'. The idea of a suffering God is exclusive to Christianity; it is not found in any other religion. Buddha, for example, appears before us as someone with a cold, priestly gaze: with his arms crossed, he communicates an immense sensation of distance and impassiveness. What a contrast with the Christ of the cross! 'A man of sorrows, and familiar with suffering ... he was pierced for our transgressions, he was crushed for our iniquities' (Isaiah 53:3, 5).

Discovering God's own pain in my suffering is a decisive step in dealing with the thorn. If suffering in the world makes faith in God difficult, God's suffering with me transforms my faith into something revolutionary. However, this is not something that can be understood only with the head, a mere idea; it is a personal and irreplaceable experience that transforms the heart. Author Doug Herman buried his wife, baby daughter and brother all within a few short months. In his book *What Good is God?* he shares the following: 'I was still in college when we discovered my late wife's HIV infection. Needless to say, my faith was deeply shaken ... One afternoon, entering the office of one of my professors, I slumped down in a chair across from his desk. "What's wrong, Doug?" he asked. I slid my Bible across his desk to him. "Prove to me that God is real," I said numbly. He paused for quite some time and never looked at the book. Instead, he studied my face. Then he gently leaned forward and slid the Bible back to me. "Prove it yourself," he replied. Although it felt harsh at the moment, it was one of the best pieces of advice I have ever received.'[15]

The final answer to the enigma of suffering is not found in intellectual debate but in the personal encounter with Christ suffering on the cross.

God has intervened: the cross of Christ, final answer to the enigma of evil

'What is God doing to remedy so much suffering?' This question opens wide the door for us to see the light of the gospel referred to above. In the drama of human suffering, God does not limit himself to intense empathy; rather, he has taken very concrete steps. Not only does he act like a sensitive spectator, but he is also a committed actor. Let's return to the Exodus passage: 'I have surely seen the affliction of my people . . . and have heard their cry because of their taskmasters. I know their sufferings, and *I have come down* to deliver them' (Exodus 3:7–8, ESV, emphasis mine). God has come down to Earth, incarnate in Jesus Christ.

Here lies the ultimate answer to the dilemma of suffering: at the cross of Christ. I personally make the words of John Stott my own in this regard: 'I could never myself believe in God, if it were not for the cross. The only God I believe in is the One Nietzsche ridiculed as *God on the cross*'.[16] God's identification with humanity's tragedy is perfectly expressed in the name Emmanuel, *God with us*. The Christ who today suffers with me is the same one who one day suffered the most ignominious death. Christ's sufferings, apart from their value with regard to our sin, confer upon him an unquestionable moral authority to help us. No one can accuse God of not knowing what it is to suffer: on the cross, Christ experienced human suffering at its maximum both physically and morally. No one has suffered more than he has. If someone doubts God's love or goodness, let them approach the drama on the cross. Dietrich Bonhoeffer, victim of the ignominious thorn of Second-World-War concentration camps, was quite right when he wrote, 'Only the suffering God can help.'[17]

This trust enables me to say, 'Lord, I don't know or understand *why*, but you know; you know everything, and this is what truly matters to me.' Don Carson, in *How Long, O Lord?* repeats the following question several times: 'When we suffer, there will sometimes be mystery. Will there also be faith?' And at the end he gives the answer: 'Yes, if our attention is focused more on the cross, and on the God of the cross, than on the suffering itself.'[18]

There are two more dimensions to God's intervention in suffering. These will be the focus of a detailed study in the following chapters, but, for now, a brief mention will suffice:

- God speaks to us and teaches us in suffering.
- God can transform suffering into good. He can transform absurd tragedies into purpose-filled stories.

The thorn has touched my life. And now, what can I do? There is a clear goal ahead: the **restoration** of the person. It is a long road, which will entail battles and assaults on several fronts. One of them is beyond the purpose of this book, but should at least be mentioned. It falls within **the physical–medical area, that of rehabilitation**. Everything ought to be done to change or minimize the effects of the thorn. This is legitimate, and it is God's will that we fight against the results of thorns, using all the instruments that science puts at our disposal. Hence the importance of rehabilitation in all its aspects: physiotherapy, special education, Braille education, or any other form of treatment, such as psychotherapy or prescription medicine. Acceptance, the central theme of this book, does not exclude action that leads to relief. Science and faith do not exclude, but rather complement, each other.

The following chapters are devoted to **emotional** and **spiritual** restoration: how to face the thorn realistically; how to fight against natural reactions such as anger, anxiety, low self-esteem and depression; how to reach the point of acceptance; and, above all, how to reach Paul's level of contentment, which is beautifully summarized in Joni's words:

> God's power shows up best in weak people ... And if God's strength resides in the weakest of us, if we through suffering and disappointment are being groomed for active duty on God's team, why should we complain?[19]

2 The thorn hurts: wrestling with God and oneself

... there was given me a thorn in my flesh ... to torment me
(2 Corinthians 12:7).

The pain from a blow is two-fold: there is the physical pain, which, relatively speaking, soon passes, and something that causes more pain (because it lasts much longer), i.e. the emotional pain. A blow or a slap is humiliating. In his commentary on this text, Calvin writes, 'To be buffeted is a severe kind of indignity. Accordingly, if anyone has had his face made black and blue, he does not, from a feeling of shame, venture to expose himself openly in the view of men.'[1] A blow or a slap stirs up a mixture of surprise, rage and feelings of injustice: 'Why?' and 'Why me?' Something very similar occurs with a thorn in its initial stage. In this chapter we will consider the reactions that a thorn produces, from both the emotional angle: the struggle with oneself, and the spiritual angle: the struggle with God.

I would like to emphasize that these feelings and reactions are a natural result of the thorn in its initial stages, normal and even necessary, because they become like an outlet to inner feelings, contributing in this way to the healing process. We should not suppress them or condemn the one who is experiencing them, as if these reactions were something negative or a sign of lack of faith. The person who expresses less pain when receiving a blow is no more spiritual, nor is the person who in the midst of perplexity opens their heart to God any less spiritual. 'What helped me most at the beginning was the attitude of the people in the church. They listened to me, accompanied me in my suffering. I felt understood. It's what I most needed those first months. I don't think I would have been able to bear sermons or theological explanations at the time, when what I most needed were not words but closeness, love and support,' said one believer.

We must therefore respect the initial feelings as an expression of life: one is in pain and cries simply because one is alive.

Initial reactions. Natural answers

> There is a time for everything...
> a time to weep and a time to laugh...
> a time for war and a time for peace.
> (Ecclesiastes 3:1, 4, 8)

An inflammation appears as soon as a person receives a blow.[2] This is the body's response to the blow it has suffered. Obviously, the greater the trauma, the greater the inflammation. Something similar occurs from the emotional point of view. This helps us understand some essential aspects of what happens inside us when we are struck by a thorn. Just as with a bodily inflammation, we discover that these emotional reactions fulfil a double purpose, one that is positive and even necessary.

- A defensive or protective function: the pain and swelling protect the area that is sensitive.
- An adaptation function: the pain and swelling enable the person to adapt to the new situation.

The adaptive function of these reactions is of such importance that healthcare professionals define them as **adaptation disorders** and they have their own section within psychiatry.[3] The essential characteristic of an adaptation disorder is 'the development of emotional or behavioural symptoms in response to an identifiable psychosocial stress factor ...

with noticeable discomfort or significant deterioration of social or professional activity'.[4] According to the predominant symptoms, there are as many as six different subtypes of adaptation disorder. The most common are those that accompany anxiety and/or a depressive mood. We will also include in these reactions bereavement, anger, guilt and others that are not considered adaptation disorders in the strictest sense but which form part of the process of accepting a thorn.

All these reactions may seem a nuisance, something negative that we hope passes quickly. Far from it, however! They are the natural reaction and a necessary stage for reaching the right kind of acceptance. Nonetheless, it should be emphasized that this is just an initial stage. The inflammation illustration is once again helpful. Inflammation normally has a limited duration. When the condition continues excessively and becomes chronic, it ceases to be physiological and becomes pathological. The same thing occurs in the emotional realm: *the temporary character* of these reactions is what establishes their normality. When they become prolonged, they are a dangerous germ for the mind and heart. For example, it is not wrong to be angry at the thorn, but *staying* angry can easily give way to bitterness. It is not wrong to doubt, but *dwelling* on doubts can end up producing a crisis of faith. It is not wrong to be sad, but *living* in constant affliction can lead to chronic depression.

Bereavement: 'Nothing will be like it was before'

This is the primary and original reaction. A thorn always involves loss, sometimes even 'a catalogue of losses'.[5] In this sense Shakespeare was right when he wrote that 'the essence of each pain has twenty shadows'.[6] Let us consider, for example, chronic and debilitating diseases, such as multiple sclerosis or polio; or the outcome of an accident that leaves a person in a wheelchair; or the impact on parents of a severely disabled child; or even something more frequent: diabetes that progressively affects a person's vision. In all these situations, the person, or those close to them, is deprived of something beautiful, which is snatched away from them abruptly and unexpectedly, such as the ability to care for oneself, physical mobility, bodily image, and even work. As a result, personal relationships and social status can be seriously affected. Every thorn represents a considerable wearing down of one's former condition. The feeling of loss lies at the root of the anger, anxiety and depression that later appear.

Identifying the painful losses and recognizing the need to go through a correct bereavement process is the first step towards a satisfactory recovery.[7] Unfortunately, many people do not realize that what they are facing is truly bereavement. They are not aware of the fact that they need to work through this sorrow just as if they had lost a loved one. The way in which a person faces these losses will to a great extent determine their acceptance of the thorn and their adaptation to the new situation. 'To think that I would never recover what I had lost, that I couldn't go back to my previous situation, plunged me into desperation. But suddenly I realized that my situation was not so different from that of someone else who had lost a loved one. I discovered that I was mourning because I also had lost something very dear to me: my mobility and the ability to manage on my own. To understand my loss as a mourning process helped me start on the road of fighting.' These words were spoken by a twenty-five-year-old woman who became disabled as the result of an accident.

The first phase in mourning for the loss produced by a thorn is common to other types of bereavement. **Confusion and numbness** appear:[8] 'I don't understand anything.' 'What's happening to me?' 'It's as if I were in a film – it doesn't seem real.' Perplexity, a type of emotional shock, sets in. It is like a 'natural anaesthesia' of the mind itself, protecting us from the distressing panorama we face. It is like a fog that keeps the distant landscape hidden – all the consequences of that diagnosis, of that unexpected news, of that brutal thorn. 'When they told me I wouldn't walk again, I simply couldn't react. I couldn't think or feel anything. My physical paralysis was accompanied by a mental and emotional paralysis. I felt that way for weeks. Then, little by little, I started to wake up, like someone coming back to reality after a horrible nightmare.' A similar idea was expressed by a mother after her child was born with a disability: 'When the doctor broke the news to me, I felt that a huge weight was pressing down on my body and my mind. I couldn't react. I felt paralysed for a good while.'

This numbness or shock, therefore, can be explained as an initial defence mechanism. Thorns generally come into our lives unexpectedly. No one is prepared for the severe upheaval that shakes the foundations of our personal and family lives. The effect is similar to an earthquake that leaves a house in ruins. The hours and days following the earthquake are full of utter confusion.

But, of course, not all thorns will have this phase of anaesthesia which comes with shock. Its presence and intensity will vary greatly according to the type of thorn and the way it starts.

'Then, little by little, I started to wake up, like someone returning to reality,' said the young woman mentioned earlier. Yes, the effect of the anaesthesia wears off and gives way to other reactions. And when the fog that hid the devastating landscape starts to lift, we become aware of the harsh reality. At that point, face to face with the thorn, staring right into the jaws of suffering, the reactions of fighting with oneself and with God appear most intensely. And they are expressed, above all, by way of:

- anger
- anxiety
- depression.

These reactions do not show up consecutively, but rather simultaneously, all mingling together in a maze of sensations and feelings. A correct understanding and handling of this 'maze' will open the door to curing our wounds, both emotional and spiritual.

Anger: 'It's not right; I don't deserve this'

Becoming angry is as natural a response as it is necessary. Of someone who never gets angry we say, 'They don't have blood in their veins', as if they were lifeless. Anger forms part of the defence mechanism that God has given us to face disagreeable or unjust situations. In fact, the ability to get angry forms part of divine nature. God presents himself to us as a God of wrath in the face of sin and injustice. We also see Jesus Christ, 'the image of the invisible God', becoming very angry at specific moments and expressing his anger vigorously. Of the apostle Paul it is said, 'his spirit was provoked within him as he saw that the city [Athens] was full of idols' (Acts 17:16, ESV). The absence of anger on certain occasions can even be displeasing to God. So there is a holy anger that reflects the image of God in us.

Why should we affirm that anger is a natural and necessary reaction? There are two main reasons:

The therapeutic value of anger

First of all, because anger liberates us, relieving our frustration. So it is emotionally healing. Once the person has come out of the bewilderment phase they are conscious of a harsh reality: they cannot be freed from the thorn and return to their previous state. This realization generally causes rejection and frustration that turn into rebellion and anger. Suppressing these feelings can be as negative as holding back tears when mourning a death. We all know that saying 'Don't cry' to a bereaved person goes against common sense and biblical teaching. Likewise, the person suffering from a thorn needs to express their pain as a way of protest. It is a basic emotional need which prepares us to fight better and, eventually, come to acceptance. Psychologically, the biggest hurdle to achieving acceptance is suppressed anger. So expressing anger is a good vaccination against possible complications, such as bitterness or crises of faith. If 'bitterness is solidified grief',[9] we must welcome a proper expression of anger as a natural outlet for our inner turmoil.

The metaphor of a sting or bite is a great help in understanding this idea. The danger of a sting tends to be found in the venom. If we can extract the venom, as in the case of a snake, the creature becomes harmless. Herein lies the value of expressing anger: it is like eliminating the venom of a sting.

Protest is the simplest way of expressing this inner unrest. Later on we will explore protesting to God. Here we focus on our relationship with others, particularly those closest to us, such as our family or church circle. Anger can show itself in varying ways and intensities, from simple ill humour to active aggression. Its most frequent manifestation, however, is irritability. 'He's hypersensitive, irascible, everything bothers him and you can't say anything to him,' the family says. A hallmark of this reaction is to blame others for the thorn or to complain that 'they are not treating me well'. Guilt is placed on others, especially loved ones. This obviously necessitates a great deal of understanding and patience on the part of caregivers or family members, who have to realize that such attitudes are not personal but a reaction to the situation of suffering. 'He's not attacking me – it's just a way his inner unrest shows up; this is why I do not take it personally' said the wife of a man suffering from incapacitating diabetes who yelled all day long in a permanent state of ill humour.

A word of caution here: if the person does not get past this stage it can cause family life to become very strained. All relationships become poisoned. In fact, *not* accepting a thorn is a major factor in marriage break-up. It is difficult to live with a bitter person because they end up making everyone else bitter.

Anger and protest, therefore, have their proper place in the acceptance process. I have known several cases of belated rebellion against a thorn among those who in the initial stages seemed to handle it admirably, without becoming at all upset or angry. This is somehow the reversal of the natural chronological order, making recovery more difficult. The biblical principle that there is a time for everything can certainly be applied here. We must remember that, in nature, the darkest storm is usually followed by a clear sky. Or, as the Psalmist says, 'weeping may remain for a night, but rejoicing comes in the morning' (Psalm 30:5).

The 'unutterable groaning' against the effects of Sin

> We know that the whole creation has been groaning as in the pains of childbirth right up to the present time. Not only so, but we ourselves . . . groan inwardly (Romans 8:22–23).

There is a second reason why anger is understandable: a spiritual one. It has to do with the reality of evil: in a fallen world, *any* thorn is indirectly a manifestation of Sin (capitalized and in the singular), which has affected all of nature without exception (Romans 8:18–24). We have already seen that there is not a direct cause-and-effect relationship – there are many thorns without sin and many sins with no resulting thorns – but rather an indirect consequence of living in a fractured world. Suffering in any of its forms is a strange thing in God's creation. We were not created to live in pain but in joy.

That is why it is logical to experience indignation and anger at the consequences of sin that destroy people's lives. Such a reaction, far from displeasing God, brings us closer to him, because God himself grieves with us in our suffering. Let us remember the reaction that Jesus had before the tomb of Lazarus: he wept. I do not believe that Jesus' tears were primarily due to the loss of his friend; after all, he knew that Lazarus would come to life in a short while. I am convinced that his tears were a heartfelt rejection of the devastating effects of sin – in this case, death. Roger Hurding, a British doctor who has experienced the thorn of a chronic disease, writes, 'It seems to me that it is a godly reaction to burn with anger not only at human pride, selfishness and greed, but at the tragedies that overtake humanity ... The deeply felt opposition that Jesus had to all the works of the devil is a pointer to our need for a holy anger against the destructive effects of sin and sickness.'[10]

'Be angry but do not sin': the limits of anger

We must then ask a logical question: When is anger wrong? The apostle Paul gives us the key: 'Be angry but do not sin; do not let the sun go down on your anger' (Ephesians 4:26, RSV). 'Become angry if you need to,' Paul says, but there is an essential condition for the anger not to become sin: 'do not let the sun go down on your anger'. The problem is not getting angry but *staying* angry. When anger makes its nest permanently in our hearts, it is no longer a *natural reaction* but an *attitude*. It ceases to be a spontaneous and transitory feeling and becomes a chronic state. When this occurs, anger turns into resentment and then, in time, breeds bitterness, a natural next step. These are the **toxic effects of restrained anger**. What begins as a necessary and positive reaction ends up immersing the person in an attitude of self-destruction.

Aware of this danger, the mother of a boy suffering from cystic fibrosis[11] asked me, 'And how can I know if this is happening to me?' 'When you or others around see that you are changing into a different person,' I replied. Comments such as, 'She doesn't seem the same; she's irritable, aggressive, closed in on herself. She's lost the sweetness she used to have', are indicators of the toxic effects of anger.

This principle applies not only to situations where we suffer from a thorn but to any relationship in which there is an element of anger. There are people who specialize in making resentment 'preserves' – storing up anger in their hearts until they are filled to the brim with bitterness and succumb to a paranoid vision of life, thinking that everything and everyone is against them. According to some historians, the secret of Nelson Mandela's great influence in his country can be summarized in one sentence: *he refused to hate or to become embittered*. What a beautiful summary of a man's life; his thorn – twenty-seven years in prison – not only failed to destroy him, but stimulated his courage and his hope of a multiracial South Africa.

'Search your hearts and be silent': putting out the fire of anger

Anger is like a fire that needs to be carefully controlled; otherwise, it can cause serious trouble. We have seen some of its dangers. The author of Proverbs warns us that 'a quick-tempered man does foolish things' (Proverbs 14:17). It is interesting to observe that the text considered earlier (Ephesians 4:26) is a quotation of Psalm 4:4: 'In your anger do not sin; when you are on your beds, search your hearts and be silent.'

The original verse, therefore, points out a need to temper anger with periods of reflection and silence. Such moments are like drops of water that quench the land razed by fire. It will be during these moments that we will meet the God who suffers with us, the God who knows our anguish and the Christ who is at our side interceding for us. We will hear the gentle voice of the Almighty asking us, as he asked Jonah, 'Do you do well to be angry?' (Jonah 4:4, RSV). It will be precisely during these hours of meditation that we will discover shafts of light in our darkness. These 'discoveries' will gradually calm the intensity of our anger and prepare us to accept the thorn.

In silence and meditation we will experience, as Teresa of Calcutta put it:

> The fruit of silence is prayer
> The fruit of prayer is faith
> The fruit of faith is love
> The fruit of love is service
> The fruit of service is peace.[12]

Anxiety: occupied or preoccupied?

> Apart from other things, there is the daily pressure on me of my anxiety for all the churches (2 Corinthians 11:28, ESV).

> Do not be anxious about anything... (Philippians 4:6).

Anxiety is another natural response in the initial stages of a thorn. Some uncertainty and insecurity regarding the future seems logical when everything is dark and bleak. In fact, there is a type of anxiety that operates like a valuable stimulus in life, including the Christian life, because it motivates us. It impels us to *occupy ourselves* appropriately with people or situations that need attention. An example of this positive concern is found in Paul's attitude towards the churches in the text of 2 Corinthians 11:28. The word used here – *merimna* – is the one Jesus used in Matthew 6:25 to condemn a certain kind of anxiety. As we will see later, the problem lies not in anxiety itself but in its *content*, that which *preoccupies* us, and in the attitudes surrounding it.

In its positive sense, anxiety caused by a thorn becomes a force that will enable us to make decisions and take the necessary steps to face the difficulty better. Until now we have referred to the adaptive value of anxiety, 'good anxiety' that is a necessary tool in the struggle against the thorn.

However, it is one thing to be *occupied* and quite another to be *preoccupied*. In its most popular sense, anxiety carries with it the idea of an excessive preoccupation regarding the future, bordering on fear, which can erode and even paralyse our ability to fight. *'What is going to happen to me? What will become of my life? How is this disease going to develop? Will I be able to work? Will I be able to earn enough to provide for my family? Who will care for this little one when we, the parents, are no longer here?'* An endless list of uncertainties rain down on our minds. Insecurity and fear dominate our thoughts in a vicious circle. It is as if the world were tumbling down on us and crushing us. The word *anxiety*, and its close relative *anguish*, come from the root word *ang*, and they convey the idea of straits, a narrow pass, something that constricts or asphyxiates. We must combat this kind of anxiety from the beginning because it cripples us in our progress towards acceptance.

Good and bad anxiety: being anxious versus toiling

As with other emotional problems, it is important to have a clear understanding of the biblical teaching on anxiety. Mistaken concepts are frequently the cause of unjust feelings of guilt. So we must make a distinction between *being anxious* and *toiling*. Not only are they different terms, but conceptually too they reflect different realities.

The anxious personality: psychological anxiety

This has to do with *a way of being*, a personality trait, which has a clear genetic base.[13] It is normally transmitted from parents to offspring through inheritance or learning (emotional 'contagiousness' when children observe the anxious behaviour of parents). Such people worry disproportionately about everything; their minds are filled with clouds of ill omen. They are specialists in 'terriblizing' – always imagining the very worst in any situation. They can never relax completely because when they have sorted out one worry they are already thinking about the next one.

The anxious personality is a psychological make-up that can, if needed,[14] be improved through cognitive therapy techniques, i.e. learning to think positively (see chapter 3). This kind of anxiety is not a sin because *it is not incompatible with trust in God*. David himself wrote, 'When I am afraid, I will trust in you' (Psalm 56:3), showing how both feelings may coexist. Later on we will see in more detail how Jacob, Moses and Jeremiah, men of great faith, passed through periods of anxiety. In the midst of their *anguish*, however, they continued to trust God in an admirable way.

'Do not be anxious about tomorrow': existential anxiety
Contrary to the previous anxiety, this is a *reaction* of mistrust towards the future, especially with regard to life's essentials: food, health and clothing, just as Jesus points out in the Sermon on the Mount (Matthew 6:25–31). The verb *merimnaō* appears up to four times in the text and gives the idea of being very worried, overwhelmed to the point of disquietude and being troubled. It is the same word that Jesus used to reproach Martha's attitude: '. . . *you are anxious and troubled* (Luke 10:41, ESV).

This kind of anxiety is clearly rebuked in the Bible because at its root is a lack of trust in God's provision. In practice, it implies denying two basic attributes of God's character: his faithfulness and his providence. It makes God a small God. No longer is he the Almighty, but rather a 'pocket-God'. If the previous form of anxiety was a psychological problem that requires treatment, existential anxiety is a sin that requires repentance. Its best treatment, as we will consider later, lies in exclaiming our full assurance with the Psalmist: But I trust in you, O Lord, . . . My times are in your hands' (Psalm 31:14–15).

Stress, the price of adapting to change

Stress, defined as a state of pressure or tension, is a frequent reality for the person suffering from a thorn. In fact, the concept of the thorn that we are using is very close to the noun *stressor* that is used in psychiatry, which shows the close relationship between both realities. The struggle against our thorns generates a tremendous amount of stress, which can occur along three different tracks:

Stress due to change

At the beginning, we said that a thorn is like a blow or an earthquake in a person's life, producing major changes. It is down this 'change' track that the harmful effect of stress penetrates. Actually, stress is measured by the changes – in quality and in quantity – that a person's life events generate.[15] Each significant event is going to cause stress in direct proportion to the degree of change produced: the greater the change, the greater the stress. This explains the consequent need for personal and social readjustment following the impact, something that will require an extra 'amount' of emotional energy, which causes the *pressure* or stress. Hence the great need to facilitate the *adaptation* to the new situation.[16]

Stress due to added burdens

'As if life were not already complicated enough, now this tragedy … Nobody can imagine the number of hours and the money and energy I have spent on my problem.' These words remind us of the woman in the gospel who suffered for twelve years from a vexing thorn, a continual discharge of blood, and who 'had spent all her living on physicians' (Luke 8:43, ESV). The pain of the thorn and its consequences had put her in desperate financial straits. Any thorn, but particularly a chronic or incapacitating disease, can be an endless source of work and extra expense. Specialized care, endless medical visits, and the adaptation to new material needs, all cause the person and their family to strive to alleviate the effects of the stressor situation; their lives revolve around the thorn. This produces wear and tear and can be exhausting for anyone. Let me emphasize here the tremendously valuable help of friends and the church family in practical and often insignificant tasks: from minding children one afternoon a week to cooking meals once in a while, help providing respite from the daily burdens brings great relief amid the stress.

Post-traumatic stress

This affects only those whose thorn began traumatically: through an accident, a natural catastrophe, an act of violence, or whatever. The symptoms form what is known as Post-traumatic Stress Disorder

(PTSD), which is characterized by the repeated reliving of the stressor experience, as if watching a film over and over again. 'It's as if in my mind I keep seeing a video of that moment and I can't stop it.' Certain images and memories are introduced as flashes in the brain, undesirable and uncontrollable, causing a high level of anxiety. It is just like going through the trauma again with its full force of anguish. In the long run, this causes emotional fatigue which is added to the stress of the thorn itself. Normally this disorder fades with time, but, if it does not, it requires professional help.

Depression: 'Life is not worth living'

> Be merciful to me, O LORD, for I am in distress;
>   my eyes grow weak with sorrow,
>   my soul and my body with grief.
> My life is consumed by anguish
>   and my years by groaning;
> my strength fails because of my affliction,
>   and my bones grow weak.
> (Psalm 31:9–10)

David was not lacking in thorn-producing situations in his life. But, in many of his psalms, we find the self-portrait of a man who knew how to wait on God in the midst of them. Little wonder, then, that many believers have found an unfailing source of comfort and encouragement in an attentive reading of the psalms, truly priceless jewels for people suffering from a thorn. When David wrote Psalm 31, a tremendous declaration of trust, he was in a very painful situation: serious family problems had culminated in the rebellion of his son Absalom, who pursued him, trying to kill him. It is hard to imagine a father facing a more difficult situation – a lacerating thorn that stabs the deepest part of the soul. This family drama lasted several years, throughout which time David experienced depression a number of times.

To what kind of depression are we referring? The mood disorder that arises from a thorn is not, at least in its initial stages, a depression in the clinical sense. It is a variant of adaptive disorders that is characterized, above all, by a state of discouragement and sadness that can turn on occasions to weeping. Actually, the correct term for it would be a

depressive reaction (or a reactive depression). It is one more of the 'inflammatory' effects of the initial blow. This is why it can be classified as foreseeable – as normal as bereavement following a significant loss.

I remember my own experience when I became aware of the seriousness of my eye problem. Indeed, I will never forget the day I arrived home after a visual field test had indicated a notable deterioration in my vision. I wept, and I wept profusely. It was short, but intense. I felt broken and needed to express the pain in my heart. I can think of nothing that would have relieved me more at that time than the tears I shed, surrounded by my loved ones. During the following weeks, feelings of hopelessness, pessimism and very low spirits were my undesired companions. Then, little by little, the depressive reaction lifted. The acceptance process was on its way.

This is not a book about depression. However, we do need to clarify some concepts, even if only briefly, just as we have done with anxiety. Those of us who have contact with sufferers of a thorn ought to know some basic biblical principles, without which we can fall into the error – the sin – of Job's friends, whom God reproached with, '... you have not spoken of me what is right' (Job 42:7).

Can a Christian feel depressed?

Many sincere believers associate depression with sin. They wonder why this modern emotional plague affects so many, including committed and mature believers. Is not Christ 'the best doctor and prayer the best therapy?'[17]

It is difficult for them to understand how a person with faith can go through periods with a depressed spirit, exhaustion or spiritual dryness. They are unable to reconcile Paul's exhortation, 'Rejoice in the Lord always', with the reality of seeing men and women of faith suffering from depression. And their perplexity is even greater when the sufferer is a spiritual leader, a pastor in the church.

Saints, but depressed!

The Word of God sheds much light on those suffering from some kind of depression and offers them real comfort. Patriarchs and prophets frequently went through the narrow pass in the valley, sometimes in the form of a depression (Elijah in 1 Kings 19:1–18; Jeremiah in chapter 20 of Jeremiah), and at other times in the form of doubt (Habakkuk, John the

Baptist), nearly always accompanied by deep experiences of loneliness and frustration (David in the Old Testament, Paul in the New).

When we see a long list of heroes of the faith passing through dark tunnels of emotional trials, our eyes are opened to an obvious conclusion: these men and women were indeed spiritual giants, but they were also flesh and blood, 'of like passions (sufferings) with us' (James 5:17, ASV). God, in his mysterious sovereignty, uses vessels of clay and not of gold. And this, really, is the central argument of this book: God allows shadows in his best vessels so that only his name will shine forth, because his 'power is made perfect in weakness . . . For when I am weak, then I am strong' (2 Corinthians 12:9–10).

Identifying depression

If depression is presented very naturally in the Bible, what then are the most frequent symptoms that appear following the arrival of a thorn? Symptoms can vary, from simply feeling discouraged to actually wanting to die. In general, a thorn produces a sense of loss in three areas, forming a characteristic triad. In each of these areas we find the symptoms of depression:

1. Loss of one's own identity: 'I'm a nobody', expressed in:

   - Feelings of inferiority: *'I'm not worth anything as a person. I feel useless.'* When suffering from a thorn, one's self-concept is at its lowest ebb and needs special attention. This is one of the problems most resistant to improvement. In fact, feelings of inferiority can persist for a long time, even after the depressive reaction has disappeared. These feelings are closely related to the losses already mentioned. To rebuild self-esteem and re-establish the person's identity is one of the key tasks in the entire recovery process and goes far beyond the initial phases.
   - Feelings of inability: *'I give up; I can't go on.'* This is due to the exhaustion brought about by unceasing wear and tear. A person says, *'My energy has run out,'* as if they were a battery. Later on we will see how this was the cause of Moses' depression.
   - Dejection, sadness, demoralization, the desire to cry. Feeling down or low tends to be the most visible symptom to outside

observers (family and caregivers), but is neither the most serious nor the most persistent symptom.

- Guilt. Those who blame themselves are unjustified in doing so, more often than not. Groundless feelings of guilt are a typical symptom of depression, as we will see later in Ana's testimony: she blamed herself for the malformations of her baby. Exceptionally, when the thorn is the direct result of an accident or event in which personal liability is involved, specific psychological treatment for guilt is needed. It is important that these feelings be alleviated to prevent the depression from lingering.

2. Loss of purpose in life: 'There's no reason for my being here':

- Indifference to life. *'Life is not worth living. I'd be better off dead.'* In serious cases, there can be suicidal tendencies. The threat of suicide is a serious complication in progressive and/or disabling diseases, especially in their initial phases when the denial reaction is very intense. Contrary to popular belief, a significant percentage of individuals who talk about harming themselves end up doing so.
- Loss of interest in everyday tasks, apathy. It is difficult to start any task, especially getting up in the morning, which is generally the worst hour of the day. This is accompanied by the loss of the ability to anticipate and experience pleasure (anhedonia), including sexual pleasure.
- Isolation. The person isolates themselves, preferring to be alone and not see or talk to anyone. They do not want to leave the house. In the most serious cases, they do not even want to get out of bed.

3. Loss of hope: 'There's no future left for me':

- Pessimism. Negative thoughts about the future. Everything seems to be under a dark cloud. Hopelessness.
- Irritability and even hostility, to the point of causing tension in relationships. Interaction can become difficult, as mentioned earlier.

When depression does not improve, it may generate further problems, such as an **addiction** to alcohol or other drugs, including psychotropic drugs or analgesics. 'When I saw that I couldn't come out of my cave, the only way to relieve my anguish was by running away. That's how I started to drink, until I realized that alcohol had become another prison, trapping me even more strongly than my thorn.' **Substance abuse** is a complication to bear in mind in situations of chronic suffering.

So far, we have described these five initial reactions as natural and necessary. But we cannot conclude this section without addressing an important question: **how long do they last?** What is considered a normal duration? This will vary greatly from one person to another for reasons involving the individual's personality, as well as the circumstances and gravity of the thorn. Something quite similar occurs with the resolution of a bereavement process. But, in general, it is accepted that these adaptive disorders last between six and twelve months. However, the recurring nature of many thorns causes a relapse in reactions each time the thorn appears. Each recurrence can be followed by a repetition of the adaptation disorders, albeit less intense and less lengthy. A certain accommodation effect is therefore produced, or, to use the medical term, there is greater tolerance. It is never like the first time. It is thought that this improvement is due not only to 'having become accustomed to the thorn', but also to the individual's personal growth in accepting it. As I said earlier, this is the teleological meaning of these reactions – i.e. their reason for being: to facilitate the adaptation to the thorn's new reality.

Even more important is the *resolution* of these disorders, i.e. that all the symptoms abate. In the same way that an inflammation fades little by little until it disappears, these initial reactions cannot become chronic, at least not in their initial form and with their initial intensity. If this happened, the acceptance process would become blocked and give way to the complications already described: bitterness, chronic depression and serious spiritual crises.

Wrestling with God

Three times I pleaded with the Lord to take it away from me.

As I ponder the mystery of unanswered prayer, I also learn simply to wait.[18]

So far we have looked at the inner struggle, the emotional reaction in the mind of the sufferer and how it affects their mood and even their personality. Let us now move on from the psychological to the spiritual realm: how do my emotional reactions affect my relationship with God?

If there is one thing that characterizes the initial stages of a thorn, it is struggle: against one's own feelings and against adverse circumstances, and also the *spiritual struggle*. It would be naïve to think that the 'inflammation' would leave our faith unscathed. Human beings are a whole in which all of our parts – body, mind, and spirit – remain inseparably joined. When one part suffers, the other parts are also affected. The stab of a thorn, whatever its nature, influences our spiritual health. No one can pretend to have a faith so lofty that 'nothing human' will affect it. Not even the Lord Jesus himself lived free from anxiety and sadness during his earthly life, especially before the supreme thorn of dying on the cross.

So, how must we face this spiritual battle? What are its dangers? And, above all, what weapons do we have to aid us?

Let us consider Paul's reaction to his thorn. At first sight, the apostle did what most of us would have done. He asked God more than once to have the thorn removed. But was it as simple as that? A superficial reading of the text can give us the impression that everything went well for Paul and that his only setback was that the Lord did not answer affirmatively. If we think this, we have missed the most important part: that the apostle's spiritual battle was long, intense and possibly never finished, since the thorn was repetitive or sporadic in nature. Two details from the text reinforce the interpretation of a prolonged struggle:

- The expression 'three times', according to many commentators, has the meaning of 'numerous times' and cannot be taken literally. In all probability it was not three but many times. For example, this is Calvin's interpretation: 'Here, also, the number three is employed to denote frequent repetition.'[19]
- In the original, the word 'pleaded' has the very strong meaning 'to entreat or to appeal earnestly and with urgency'. 'Three times I pleaded with the Lord to take it away from me' (1 Corinthians 12:8). We can imagine Paul praying fervently, kneeling before the Father numerous times, until he clearly understands the divine answer. We do not know how much time passed between his first

prayer and God's answer. Maybe the Lord answered him right from the start, but the text does not give us the details. On the other hand, we can deduce from the phrase 'he said to me' (v. 9) that it was a repeated answer – and not just once – in logical correlation with the *'numerous times'* Paul had prayed. We could therefore paraphrase the text this way: 'Many times I have prayed, pleading with the Lord to take the thorn away from me, but he always answered me saying . . .'. As we shall see in chapter 5, a number of important and practical implications with regard to the need for an ongoing relationship with Christ, and our dependence on him in our fight against the thorn, stem from this.

Prayer is the right attitude when facing thorns, but frequently it will be neither an easy nor a brief experience. Rather, it will be a struggle, like that of Paul, and of numerous other men and women in the Bible, who, overcome with doubt, sought God sincerely in the midst of situations of suffering or great need. Common to all these people was an intense desire for a divine answer to their earnest prayers.

Such was the case with Hannah, the prophetess and mother of Samuel, who, burdened by her infertility (a frequent thorn for many couples today), emptied her heart out before God asking him for a son: 'she kept on praying to the LORD' (1 Samuel 1:12). We glimpse the intensity of Hannah's praying through the mistaken deduction of Eli that she was drunk. In this case, God's answer was affirmative and the woman's expression of gratitude is one of the most beautiful prayers in the entire Bible (1 Samuel 2).

Let us now consider the case of two Bible characters whose thorns led them to wrestle with God: Jacob and Jeremiah.

Jacob, the man who fought with God and won
The expression 'wrestling with God', at the head of this chapter, is literally the story of Jacob at Peniel. The long and conflictual relationship with his brother, Esau, enables us to include it in the category of suffering from a thorn. Jacob had lived for many years with the uncertainty caused by his brother's death threat (Genesis 27:41). Now, one night, in the valley of Jabbok, the moment of truth had arrived. Deeply worried about the imminent re-encounter with Esau, he felt 'great fear and distress' (32:7). Jacob sought God with great intensity, first

through the beautiful prayer in Genesis 32:9–12. Then later, all night long, he wrestled openly with 'a man' – God himself, it transpired – until he obtained the blessing he so greatly desired: 'Because you have struggled with God and with men and have overcome' (32:28). This blessing meant renewed certainty that God was with him, just as Jacob had been promised at another memorable encounter in Bethel several years earlier: 'I am with you and will watch over you wherever you go, and I will bring you back to this land. I will not leave you until I have done what I have promised you' (Genesis 28:15).

Victor, but lame. The story of Jacob's thorn, however, does not end with triumphalism. We notice the double effect of his wrestling with God. On the one hand, he went away greatly *blessed*, for God had given him a new identity – 'Your name will no longer be Jacob, but Israel'. (Certainly this is the main point of the story: the renewal of his covenant relationship with God that had started some years earlier at Bethel.) On the other hand, he also went away *injured*, bearing the sign of a limp, which accompanied him for the rest of his life: '[The man] touched the socket of Jacob's hip so that his hip was wrenched as he wrestled with the man ... The sun rose above him as he passed Peniel, and he was limping because of his hip' (Genesis 32:25b, 31).

This may seem a minor detail compared with the rich theological meaning and the purpose of the whole passage. But I find this 'minor' personal event in Jacob's life very relevant to our topic. God freed him from a thorn: the hatred of and pursuit by his brother, but now a new thorn appears: his dislocated hip – certainly not a trivial problem because it made his life more difficult in practical terms. A limp like this was a serious handicap in a nomadic society, where it was essential to be able to move about nimbly in order to survive. Surely it was not God who had caused Jacob to become lame, but indeed he allowed the disability and he used it. In which way? By permitting the patriarch to become lame immediately before his encounter with Esau, (humanly speaking) God deprived him of his main means of defence, that of being able to run away. He was completely subject to his brother's will. God used this new thorn to teach the patriarch the same lesson that Paul had to learn: God's power reaches its highest splendour in weakness. A lame Jacob had no other choice but to trust God fully. Deprived of his natural resources, he depended completely on God's supernatural resources: his power and grace.

Jeremiah: the prophet who knew how to face his doubts

One of the great dangers is that the sting of a thorn can affect our faith. Suffering does not always cause us to draw closer to God – at least not initially. Sometimes it has the opposite effect, leaving us so perplexed that it causes us to doubt everything, including our firmest beliefs. 'Where is God's goodness?' we ask ourselves. Is faith maybe an illusion? Why does God seem so distant?' If you feel like this, you are thinking no differently from some of the giants of faith. David, for example, frequently exclaimed, 'How long, O LORD? Will you forget me for ever?' (Psalm 13:1). 'Hear my prayer, O LORD, listen to my cry for help; be not deaf to my weeping' (Psalm 39:12). Even John the Baptist, of whom the Lord said, 'Among those born of women there has not risen anyone greater than John the Baptist' (Matthew 11:11), oppressed by his imprisonment and imminent death, came to doubt Jesus' identity and asked, 'Are you the one who was to come, or should we expect someone else?' (Luke 7:19). In times of crisis God can seem far away, absolutely silent, and everything seems to be caving in. This is fertile ground for the doubts that start to thrive like thistles in the field of belief.

How do we prevent these incipient doubts from causing our faith to run aground and sink? The key is to face them squarely. The illustration of a snake or stinging insect is appropriate here. After being injured, we have to do everything possible to get the venom out. When a thorn strikes us the worst thing we can do is close in on ourselves even more, ignoring the questions that rise out of our perplexity, immersed in a silence that reflects a false acceptance. Suppressing the doubts is like storing the snake's venom, for sooner or later its poison will end up injuring us. The author and speaker Os Guinness starts his excellent book on doubt[20] with a chapter entitled 'I Believe in Doubt'. This may seem a contradiction, but it contains a great truth: in the measure that we are able to understand the meaning and nature of doubts, even their healthy value as inducers of faith, we will lose our fear and be able to face them correctly.

For this reason, Jeremiah serves very well as an example. We can easily identify with the so-called 'weeping prophet' and his apparent 'fights' with God. His ups and downs are a mirror reflecting the spiritual life of many believers struggling against a thorn.

What was **Jeremiah's thorn**? In fact, he had several, but I'm high-lighting one: his absolute loneliness in the midst of such great opposition that it even took him to his death. Why *absolute* loneliness? Because it affected his entire being. It was an emotional, a spiritual and even a physical loneliness: everyone had abandoned him. He had no family – he could not have wife or children (Jeremiah 16:1–2); he was relentlessly pursued even by his friends (20:10); he was slandered and insulted (20:7b); he was impoverished to the point of losing all his possessions (12:7–8). Surely, Jeremiah had every right to exclaim, 'No one understands me, no one supports me, everyone has left me, and my life has no meaning or purpose.' And so much effort for what? His prophetic ministry bore no fruit – a complete failure in spite of the high cost he had paid.

His thorn was the result of his faithful obedience to God, as impressively described in chapter 20, one of the most striking lament prayers in the Old Testament. As we saw in chapter 1, some thorns are the direct result of obeying the Lord fully. And this was the case with Jeremiah.

A key aspect of this prophet's life was his relationship with God, a loving relationship that was at the same time interspersed with protest and laments. Frequently his faith entered a crisis period because he did not understand certain aspects of the divine will, but it wasn't 'weak faith', far from it, for it was his strong faith that enabled him to be – in God's own words – like 'a fortified city, an iron pillar and a bronze wall' (Jeremiah 1:18). A strong faith, however, does not preclude ups and downs, times of perplexity before the mysteries of providence. The questions Jeremiah asked echo with many believers today. *'Why? How long? Where is God when he allows these things to happen?'* His prayers sometimes became fiery protests. He threw the entire weight of his heart on the Lord. In his vehement complaints he used judicial language: 'I bring a case before you' (Jeremiah 12:1). Is there anything wrong with this? Isn't doubting sin?

Doubt your doubts: how to prevent a faith crisis
What can we learn from Jeremiah's sincere prayers in which he poured out all his questions to the Almighty? Among the many lessons, there are five that can particularly help us:

- Jeremiah's doubts were born of perplexity, the fruit of an afflicted heart. Some doubts are born of unbelief; they are the fruit of a haughty mind and a hardened heart, like the doubts of an atheist.

This was not the case with Jeremiah. The prophet protests, but always from the position of faithfulness to and trust in God; even in his darkest moments, when his faith seems to be in crisis, he is on the Lord's side. And we find not a single reprimanding word from God.

- Doubts that are born of perplexity are the sign of spiritual life. Logically, doubt cannot exist without previous belief. A comparison with physical pain can help us understand this: a dead person cannot feel pain; only a living person can feel pain. In this respect, far from being negatives, questions and doubts encourage the believer's growth and help create his or her own spiritual defences. Someone who has never had questions about their faith is at risk of having a very weak spiritual 'immune system'.

- Jeremiah did not complain about God, but to God. The difference is important. It is not sin to tell God how we feel because he is more pleased with the honesty of a bold prayer than with the coldness of a proud heart. Sin lies in defying God, not in protesting to him. We must remember the original meaning of the verb 'to protest', which is 'to declare before someone'.

- To express a doubt is positive and necessary because it prevents greater ills. This refers, of course, to doubt born of tribulation. Although it may seem paradoxical, this is the best way to avoid having a crisis of faith. You don't have to be a psychologist to see the therapeutic value of *katharsis* – sharing or unloading those emotions or thoughts that weigh us down. Impression without expression easily leads to depression.

- It is not wrong to doubt, but it is to linger in doubt; hence the importance of *making known* and not *hiding* the doubts born of a troubled heart. It is like a dirty wound. The worst thing we can do is to cover it without first cleaning it well, thereby risking infection. Hiding our doubts is like covering an uncleaned wound. In this case, the equivalent of infection is a spiritual crisis, and many people have seen their faith dwindle away due to their deficient treatment of this type of doubt. The best antidote for a crisis of faith is to air our doubts, discussing them with someone who can understand and give us answers. That is what Jeremiah did, as he had learned that protesting is not incompatible with drawing near to the Lord.

A lover's conflict: Jeremiah does not fight against God but seeks God

At first sight, Jeremiah is in conflict with God, his complaints apparently expressing more rebelliousness than trust. However, that is not so. It is helpful here to understand a psychological phenomenon that occurs in relationships with our loved ones, for example between a couple or between parents and children. Every conflict shrouds a double message. On the one hand, there is the confrontation, the negative side of the protest. When two people have an argument, the first reaction is to think that they are one *against* the other.

However, there is something deeper. I do not argue or fight with someone to whom I am indifferent. If that were the case, I would simply ignore that person. A conflict contains the non-verbal message 'You matter to me. I need you to say something to me'. What is really being sought through the conflict is for the two parties to get closer to each other. This is what happens between many married couples: very often, their arguments do not arise from rejection, but out of the love that is already there. The couple are not seeking to distance themselves from each other but to draw nearer. The worst thing that can exist in a love relationship is the silence that comes from indifference, not the conflict that comes from the desire to draw closer.

Jeremiah complained to God because he needed and wanted to come nearer to him and know his answer. He was not struggling *against* God but *in search* of God. It is the struggle of someone who loves, not the struggle of an atheist or a sceptic. If Jeremiah had not cared at all about the divine message, he would not have fought God, but would simply have been indifferent or disobeyed him. This is why the Lord never condemns the sincere expression of doubts and feelings of perplexity that spring from a heart oppressed by hardship and pain.

When you find yourself filled with doubts and questions, remember these words, which have always brought me much comfort:[21]

> Doubt your doubts and believe your beliefs; but never believe your doubts nor doubt your beliefs.

Stones along the road: overcoming despondency and exhaustion

One of the greatest problems with Paul's thorn was its recurring or repetitive nature. This is understood from the phrase 'to torment me' ('to buffet me', NKJV), since the verb is in the present tense. As we have already seen, it was not a single experience, but rather it continued to buffet him periodically or constantly.

The struggle against the thorn is a long-distance race, a marathon that wears the runner down and brings with it serious dangers. These are the stones that Satan places along the road in order to hinder our progress towards acceptance and adaptation. Two stand out because of their frequency: *despondency* and *exhaustion*. When these reactions are intense they can cause clinical depression. This was what happened to Moses. Numbers 11:11–15 is an excellent summary of what we have considered up to this point of the chapter. We are going to see embodied in Moses, this great leader of Israel, the struggle with himself and with God due to an unusual thorn.

Moses, the leader who wanted to die

People at times are the cause of a thorn. We have already seen how some have interpreted Paul's problem along these lines, attributing the thorn to Alexander the metalworker or to Hymenaeus and Philetus, who were difficult people, a source of constant pain and worry to the apostle. Indeed, there are people who are so difficult to live and work with that they can completely sap the energy and patience of the greatest saints. And this was Moses' experience. God had chosen him to guide the people of Israel: what a noble and beautiful task, to shepherd God's flock! But a relationship spanning so many years with 'a stiff-necked people' (Deuteronomy 9:6, 13), who were disobedient and murmured unceasingly, became an unbearable thorn for the meek patriarch. At times this caused him to lose control, allowing himself to be overcome by irritability (an unequivocal symptom of emotional exhaustion), as happened at Meribah, when Moses struck the rock twice instead of speaking to it, as the Lord had commanded him (Numbers 20:8–13; Psalm 106:32–33). On another occasion he could not restrain his anger against the people's idolatry, and he broke the tablets of the law into pieces (Exodus 32:19).

Tired of putting up with the people's sin and complaints, Moses was well used to discouragement. One of his crises was so intense that he reached the point of wanting to die. Overwhelmed by the weight of the responsibility he bore, feeling alone and exhausted, his spirit grew weak:

He asked the LORD, 'Why have you brought this trouble on your servant? What have I done to displease you that you put the burden of all these people on me? . . . I cannot carry all these people by myself; the burden is too heavy for me. If this is how you are going to treat me, put me to death right now – if I have found favour in your eyes – and do not let me face my own ruin' (Numbers 11:11, 14–15).

Here we find a great man of faith – of whom it is said 'he persevered because he saw him who is invisible' (Hebrews 11:27) – in the dark tunnel of depression.

The symptoms of Moses' depression

In an initial stage of depression, Moses addresses God, apparently making him accountable for the way he had acted, even censuring God for having called him to this task. There are plenty of *'whys'* that reflect the protest and confusion of the great leader. He asks God as many as five questions (vv. 11–13), all of them revealing a clearly depressed spirit. He feels he has been harmed and ill treated, feelings typical of depression, when the mind distorts facts and reality is imagined as being much worse than it is.

Moses needs freely to pour out everything in his heart. This is therapeutic because, as we saw earlier, the expression of one's thoughts and emotions has a remarkable liberating effect. Moses cannot contain himself. He needs to get rid of the anger and frustration that have built up in his heart. His words, and especially his manner and tone, reveal the level of his irritability. It is worth noting that Moses, considered 'more humble than anyone else on the face of the earth' (Numbers 12:3), reached this extreme point. His weariness and harsh – almost hostile – words against the people reveal exhaustion and disappointment. He had no strength left to continue.

The patriarch's protest reaches its greatest intensity in 11:12: 'Did I conceive all these people? Did I give them birth? Why do you tell me to carry them in my arms, as a nurse carries an infant?' We sense Moses' desire to abandon everything. He 'hands in his resignation to God'. Nevertheless, his emotional unloading starts to bear fruit in the next verse, where he is able to articulate a more reasoned and concrete complaint: 'Where can I get meat for all these people?'

Just like Jeremiah, when Moses emptied his heart and presented his burdens to God, *he did not complain about or against God but to God*. Even in the midst of his depression, he talks to God from a position of submission and loyalty. It is not sin to tell God how we feel, even if our protest is as vehement as that of Moses.

Another typical symptom of depression is distorted thinking. Our capacity for reasoning and perceiving reality is deeply altered and we see everything from a pessimistic and hopeless viewpoint. Negative thoughts appear forcefully in this Bible passage. Confused by his depressive outlook, Moses was mistaken in his assessment of God and in the evaluation of his own work. He thought God had abandoned him and even wanted to do him harm. The prophet felt that he himself had been a complete failure.

The crisis builds to a crescendo, culminating in verse 15 with his thoughts of death: 'If this is how you are going to treat me, put me to death right now.' The process is quite logical. His ideas of failure, uselessness and even unjustified guilt lead Moses to feel that he is in a cul-de-sac: only death would free him. He first directs his complaint against God, then against the people, and finally against himself. The tension has become unbearable: the patriarch has lost his self-esteem, a key factor in any depression, and this leads to loss of hope. The only 'solution' is death.

Some sufferers of apparently unbearable thorns can go through a similar experience: there is no exit to be seen and they want to die. We must remember that, in these situations, suicidal ideas are the result of a sick mind that is incapable of thinking anything positive. The person's thinking is twisted and dislocated; the person is outside themselves. Sometimes depression is a real disease that affects the mind, feelings, and even the will, and it requires proper treatment by a professional.

The thorn of a rebellious people, the cause of his depression

Opening up his heart to God without reservation proved very beneficial to Moses, not only due to its liberating effect but also because it shed light on his problem. The confused man is now in a condition to see his own reality more clearly, to the point that he even comes to understand the scope of his depression: 'I cannot carry all these people by myself; the burden is too heavy for me' (v. 14). A brilliant diagnosis! The previous context, in verses 1 to 10, helps us to understand the reasons for his exhaustion: the repeated complaining of the people, their incessant whining, had drained even God's patience: 'And the anger of the LORD blazed hotly' (v. 10, ESV). It is not surprising, then, that the patriarch's emotional tension ends up undermining his mental strength. It is clear that Moses suffered from an **exhaustion-induced depression**.

God's answer to Moses

How does God act? Some of the following ideas will be expanded in chapter 4, when we refer to God's attitude towards Paul's thorn, but here we cannot omit the essential characteristics of the Lord's answer to Moses without leaving the exposition of the text incomplete.

> The LORD said to Moses: 'Bring me seventy of Israel's elders who are known to you as leaders and officials among the people. Make them come to the Tent of Meeting, that they may stand there with you. I will come down and speak with you there, and I will take of the Spirit that is on you and put the Spirit on them. They will help you carry the burden of the people so that you will not have to carry it alone' (Numbers 11:16–17).

In this moment of greatest need, when Moses could not do anything, and all he desired was to die, the soothing word of the Supreme Doctor comes forth. God well knew the cause of Moses' condition, and the answer came in the most appropriate fashion.

There are three aspects that need to be highlighted in the way that God operates, which are applicable not only to depression but to all the emotional reactions considered in this chapter, such as anxiety, stress and anger. In the answer God gives we find:

- **Understanding**. God did not censure Moses for his depression, nor did he treat him roughly; the Lord spoke not a single word of reproach. God appears before us as expert in giving support to and showing solidarity with the grieving person. What the patriarch needed least at that moment were words of rebuke. Humanly, it may seem to us that Moses needed some kind of correction. But God is 'a compassionate and gracious God, slow to anger, abounding in love and faithfulness' (Psalm 86:15). God's answer to Moses is a revealing warning to those who hasten to issue condemning judgments or signs of disapproval when they see another member of God's family like a 'bruised reed' or a 'smouldering wick' (Isaiah 42:3). If we want to look like our

Master, we will do well to imitate him. Mercy, understanding and empathy should be much more prevalent than severe judgment, chastisement or condemnation.

- **Practical help**. God provides a way out. God's answer is not limited to understanding his depressed servant. He actually gives him the most easily accessible help so he can come out of the depression. Moses' emotional state was quite similar to a city under enemy siege, and the most urgent thing is to find a way out that will provide relief from the siege. Note that God does not give Moses an instant 'solution' that will make the problem magically disappear. He did not change Moses for another leader or even give him the opportunity to rest. The people continued to be difficult and the responsibility of leadership did not go away. But something very important did change: God provided the appropriate tools that Moses needed: 'Seventy elders . . . will help you carry the burden of the people so that you will not have to carry it alone.' God provides the right answer at the right moment.

- **Encouragement for his self-esteem**. It is clear from the text that God did not consider Moses' depression to be wrong or a sin. If that had been the case, he would have set Moses aside from such a strategic responsibility. Someone who is living in sin cannot continue to lead the people unless there is repentance, as in David's case. God reaffirmed Moses and his task with a very therapeutic phrase: ' . . . and I will take of the Spirit that is on you and put the Spirit on them' (v. 17). Here God reveals himself as being exquisitely knowledgeable about the human mind. Had Moses not complained that God was treating him badly and that he had been practically rejected by God (v. 11)?

Moses' severely dented self-esteem needed a good dose of restoration. We must remember that feelings of inferiority are one of the key problems in the struggle against the thorn. The phrase 'I will take of the Spirit that is on you and put the Spirit on them' encouraged Moses greatly in two areas. On the one hand, God had not forgotten him. God's spirit was still with the leader of the people. On the other hand, God could not fill the other elders with a depressed and weak spirit! The logic is astounding: 'If God takes my spirit to give it to others, it must mean that I'm not such disaster as I thought!' God was ratifying his trust in him and in his work. 'Moses, I'm on your side; I continue to trust you.' This was the implicit message.

God's loving and delicate handling of the situation brought about the desired result, enabling Moses to find a way out of the dark valley of depression. Later events in his life show us that this crisis was not without fruit. A thorn is never a senseless experience.

How could Moses, David, Jeremiah and Paul keep pressing on without fainting in their struggle against their thorns? How can you and I do likewise? Let us consider, as a brief conclusion, the tools that the Lord provides to help us advance along the rocky road that leads to acceptance.

Basic equipment for the journey: trust in God

We have considered the dangers of the road, the stones that Satan uses to hinder our progress towards the goal of acceptance of the thorn. Whereas Satan places stones, God provides the right equipment for this journey. We could mention many 'garments' that we should wear, but we will emphasize two: our suitcase must contain patience and trust.

Since patience – defined as the determination to persevere – is the key, enabling us to run 'the race marked out for us' (Hebrews 12:1), we will be covering it in the final chapter. At this point we will focus on trust.

Trust lies at the core of faith because there are many things in life that we will never understand. Such situations require from us the spirit of a child who fully trusts his father or mother. God's question to us in times of trial is not *'do you understand me?'* but *'do you believe/trust me?'* Faith does not require *understanding* everything that God is doing in the world or in my life, but *believing* that he knows best what he is doing. Faith is ultimately an exercise in trusting the One who told Peter 'you do not realize now what I am doing, but later you will understand' (John 13:7).[22]

Let us take a look at how some of this chapter's protagonists – Moses, David and Jeremiah – lived, trusting the Lord completely in the midst of their thorns.

- **Moses**. The author of Hebrews reveals to us the great secret of Moses' perseverance, which enabled him to continue with his arduous task of leading the people of Israel:

'... he was looking ahead to his reward ... he persevered because he saw him who is invisible' (Hebrews 11:26–27).

From the context we see how trust is born of and fed by faith, a faith that allowed Moses to see him who is invisible – a beautiful paradox. The expression *'he persevered'* cannot be clearer: he held out because he had an unshakeable trust in his Lord. This enabled him to cling to God in the darkest hour of his depression and in other difficult moments of his relationship with the people.

- **David**. And what shall we say of David, whose thorn, as we have seen, was also caused by people? In the words of Charles Swindoll, 'I cannot think of anyone more suitable to inspire our trust in God than the psalmist David. He was hunted, haunted, and hounded by his enemies'.[23]

    Let us allow David to answer for himself, in Psalm 31:9, 14–15:

    > ... I am in distress...
    > But I trust in you, O LORD;
    >   I say, 'You are my God.
    > My times are in your hands.'

    Indeed, trust means leaving your future in God's hands and, as Jesus said, 'do not worry about tomorrow, for tomorrow will worry about itself. Let the day's own trouble be sufficient for the day' (Matthew 6:34, NIV/RSV). This confidence gives us rest beyond the afflictions of any sort of thorn and provides a totally different perspective on anxiety and depression.

- **Jeremiah**. The big secret of this prophet's life was that he struggled and fought while always clinging to God. This is what enabled him to hold out like 'a fortified city, an iron pillar and a bronze wall to stand against...' (Jeremiah 1:18). And right after that, referring to those who were Jeremiah's thorn, God declared, 'They will fight against you but will not overcome you, for I am with you and will rescue you' (1:19).

    Following the explosion of perplexity and doubt in the first part of chapter 20, we find a man who breaks out in praise to God and in a declaration of notable trust:

> But the LORD is with me like a mighty warrior . . .
> Sing to the LORD!
>   Give praise to the LORD!
> (Jeremiah 20:11, 13)

What did these three great men have in common? On the one hand, all three were *jars of clay*, weak and vulnerable in human terms. But these jars of clay became *jars of gold* in the hands of the Supreme Potter whose power is made perfect in weakness. They had learned to trust in God, the *'Rock of ages'*. They reveal to us the secret of hope that emanates from trust. Their attitude is a model and an encouragement to us as we face our own thorns with the strength of faith. If we want to emulate them, we must learn to fight while clinging to God and to wait and 'believe even against all hope' (Romans 4:18).

3 Acceptance: the key weapon for defeating the enemy

God, grant me the serenity
to accept the things I cannot change;
courage to change the things I can;
and wisdom to know the difference.[1]

'I feel like a millionaire who has lost ten pounds.' These words, spoken by a Spanish journalist in an interview after becoming tetraplegic owing to a traffic accident, made a deep impact on me and raised questions in my mind.

How can a person going through such adverse circumstances react so courageously and have such a positive attitude? We all know people who struggle in the midst of life's storms, beaten by crashing waves, who yet remain capable of delighting in the smallest details and maintaining a tough spirit and positive attitude. Their example inspires us and their determination is contagious. On the other hand, why do some people always look dissatisfied and seem to live 'drenched in a permanent complaint'? This was the case for the Romanian philosopher Emil Cioran, who even wrote a book with a very eloquent title: *Syllogisms of Bitterness*.[2] In one of his thoughts he says: 'The secret of my adaptation to life? I have changed from one type of despair to another as often as I have changed my shirt.'[3] How does one explain the difference between these two reactions? What's the secret? Can we do something to achieve a minimum level of 'happiness' in the midst of the pain caused by chronic suffering? Can we avoid bitterness when touched by the thorns of life? The answer to these questions introduces us to the climax of our study.

As I did some research on the subject, mostly through direct contact with my patients, I realized that there are two words that hold the key to helping a person grieved by a thorn: **acceptance** and **grace**. These words are in fact closely related, because, ultimately, acceptance can be achieved only by the grace of God. This is what we will call the *supernatural* ingredient of acceptance. It depends on faith and comes from God. However, there are also certain aspects that depend on us, the *natural* resources of acceptance, which are biological, psychological or environmental in nature. All of them help us decisively as we travel the long road that leads to overcoming the trauma of the thorn.

However, it must be said that even in the course of learning these human or natural aspects, we do not depend solely on ourselves; we are not alone. Nor is the outcome the exclusive result of our efforts. In fact, it is through these human resources that the grace of God starts to manifest itself in a concrete, practical way. We therefore cannot assume the arrogance of modern humanistic schools of psychology, which essentially say: 'Everything is in your hands. Your happiness depends on you. If you put your mind to it, you can triumph over any circumstance. You choose your own destiny in life.'

No, we are not little gods. We cannot, and nor do we want to, occupy the centre of our life because that place belongs to God alone. For us, as believers, the ability to overcome the thorn depends not only, nor even primarily, on the best use of our inner resources – 'the force that is in me' – but rather on the supernatural strength that comes from God, a strength that is able to transform our weaknesses into strengths. Therefore the ultimate merit when we reach a reasonable level of acceptance lies not in our own effort but in the grace of Jesus Christ. Here we can apply the phrase of Jesus: '[render] to Caesar what is of Caesar and to God what is of God'. Psychology teaches us to take advantage of these inner resources; we do our part as much as possible, but grace is the essential requisite for victory over our weaknesses.

What does it mean to accept?

Before we consider the ingredients of acceptance, we must clarify some concepts. There are many people who react negatively to the very mention of the word *accept*. Mostly the reason is that they have wrong ideas about its meaning and implications. Let's examine some of the most frequent misunderstandings.

To accept does not mean to resign oneself: the stoic-fatalist version

For many people, acceptance is the conclusion they reach when 'you can't do anything else'. You've tried everything and you've reached the end of the road. So, *'there's no alternative other than to accept'*. This is an unconditional surrender following a hard-fought battle. This idea is much closer to stoicism than to biblical teaching. As we shall see, Paul is very distant from Seneca, the main Stoic philosopher, who extolled the self-sufficiency of the individual in a manner that approached fatalism. Fatalism is born of the conviction that we can do nothing to fight against our own destiny.

Obviously, a Christian cannot agree with this position. We are not responsible for *what we have received*, but we are responsible for *what we do with what we have received*. One of the worst attitudes in the fight against the thorn is a fatalistic resignation that generates as much passivity as it does bitterness. There is a close connection between the bitterness of the person distressed by the thorn and their willingness to fight and win through. The person who is passive and doesn't lift a finger to fight has a high probability of becoming bitter and making the lives of those around them equally bitter.

To accept does not mean to put up a shield: the Eastern or Buddhist version

There are others for whom accepting means something like 'disconnecting', achieving a mental state of relaxation that approaches impassiveness: 'I don't let anything get the better of me, nor do I let anything affect me.' This idea is quite popular today because people are overwhelmed by so many kinds of thorn that they need this shell or shield in order to live more 'happily'. They are obsessed by allowing *'things to affect me as little as possible'*. It's curious to see the number of people, including top-level executives, who practise *Tai Chi* in the park early in the morning as if it were a secular 'devotional time'. Or maybe not so secular, because the common denominator of this 'shield philosophy' originates in Transcendental Meditation and other Eastern religions, particularly Buddhism. To accept does not mean to achieve a sort of *nirvana*, a supreme state that is above good and evil and in which pain disappears. In this sense acceptance becomes a kind of technique learned through systematic training. It is something like mental gymnastics.

What a contrast with the biblical idea of acceptance, a process of inner transformation born out of personal communion with the God of all grace! Far from being a cold, impersonal technique, it is an ongoing relationship with Christ for continual renewal of strength.

To accept does not imply agreement with the thorn: the masochistic version

No one asks us to be friends with the cause of our suffering. The thorn must not be seen as an enemy, but neither should it be seen as a friend. This would bring us close to a masochistic attitude, also far removed from the biblical perspective. The Lord does not ask us to 'be happy in all situations'. Paul was certainly very emphatic in saying: 'Rejoice in the Lord always. I will say it again: Rejoice!' (Philippians 4:4). But being *joyful* is not the same as being *happy*. The joy of the Lord is not so much a feeling as a profound attitude of *serenity and peace* born out of our communion with God. Hence the great paradox of the second beatitude: 'Blessed are those who mourn, for they will be comforted' (Matthew 5:4). I can be mourning the death of a loved one and have – retain – the joy that is born from considering the blessings that are mine in the Lord and which nothing and no one can take away, as Paul himself exclaims triumphantly in Romans 8:35–39. To laugh during moments of sadness is therefore not an expression of joy. God wants his children to be realists, not masochists! We are called to give thanks to God *in* all situations, but not *for* all situations.

Neither friend nor foe: an ally. To accept means to stop seeing the thorn as an enemy, as a paralysing obstacle, and to discover an ally in it. An enemy inhibits, blocks, hinders. An ally, on the other hand, helps and aids the capacity to fight. Here we are at the heart of our topic. Once we are able to understand this point, we will have advanced a long way down the road toward acceptance. *To accept means coming to the serene* *conviction that God can use my life not only in spite of my thorn, but precisely through it.* When I see the thorn as an ally, defiance gives way to acceptance. In this manner, all the energy that I previously used in fighting *against*, I can now use in fighting *for*. Before, I was immersed in a *wearing* struggle, a battle that eroded all my defences; now I discover that my ally helps me to *build* a different life, a life that is equally full and has meaning.

The ingredients of genuine acceptance

At the beginning of this chapter I pointed out that each of us faces adversity differently. Up to a certain point, these different ways of reacting form a reliable X-ray not only of our character, but also of our philosophy of life and even of our Christian maturity. In a sense, we could paraphrase the proverb 'A man is known by the company he keeps' and affirm: 'A person is known by how they react to adversity.' I am referring specifically to medium- and long-term reactions, not to the initial surprise and shock that, as we saw in the previous chapter, form part of the natural response. Thus, the experience of the thorn provides us with an excellent opportunity for discovering new facets of our character and for delving into our lives in ways that we would never have done had it not been for the experience of the thorn. Chronic suffering can be enormously energizing, from both the emotional and the spiritual viewpoint, as we will see in the next chapters. For the time being, though, let's return to the key question.

Why do people react so differently and even so paradoxically when facing the thorn? The answer introduces us to a cardinal principle: *to be happy or unhappy depends not so much on our circumstances as on our attitude in the face of those circumstances.* The ancient Greek philosopher Epictetus is supposed to have said, 'It is not the facts and events that upset man, but the view he takes of them.' However, we need to be cautious here; there are situations of chronic suffering where thorns hammer the soul until it is pierced by them, thus making headway towards acceptance difficult, sometimes very difficult indeed. We must be careful not to fall into triumphalism or into stoicism because then we will be more irritating to others than consoling. But undoubtedly the key to any adverse event lies more in the heart than in the thorn, and in the long run our attitude can be more influential and decisive than the thorn's demoralizing and devastating force. No one is destined to succumb to adversity.

Acceptance is a process of inner transformation that develops on three levels of a person. In fact, they are interdependent facets constituting a cluster, each implying a certain apprenticeship that is taking place simultaneously on three levels:

- learning to *see* differently
- learning to *think* differently
- learning to *live* differently.

Learning to see differently: contentment

I have learned to be content whatever the circumstances (Philippians 4:11).

The first ingredient of acceptance has to do with my way of looking *at* the thorn, and then *from* the thorn, i.e. the perspective that opens up following the initial shock. The person afflicted by an adverse event undoubtedly no longer sees the landscape of their life as they did before: many things have changed; sometimes, 'everything seems so different'. It is equally certain, however, that I need to discover rays of light in the darkness of this new landscape. These are unknown aspects that are opening up before my eyes and helping me to fight better or make my burden more bearable.

How can we gain a different view? The key step is to learn *contentment*. In order to study this concept in depth, let's focus on Philippians 4:11–13, where the apostle Paul presents a brilliant exposition of contentment. I have chosen this text for two reasons: firstly, because the significance of the Pauline expression 'I have learned to be content' is quite close to the modern concept of acceptance, and, secondly, because Paul is writing with a high degree of moral authority, the authority of someone himself overwhelmed with numerous burdens. In fact, he wrote this text in prison in Rome while facing the very real threat of death.

I am not saying this because I am in need, for I have learned to be content whatever the circumstances. I know what it is to be in need, and I know what it is to have plenty. I have learned the secret of being content in any and every situation, whether well fed or hungry, whether living in plenty or in want. I can do everything through him who gives me strength (Philippians 4:11–13).

The nature of contentment

What did Paul mean when he affirmed, 'I have learned to be content'? The Greek word he used – *autarkeia* – sheds much light on this: it implies not depending on, being above, the circumstances. Its emphasis lies in autonomy, in not being bound by events or problems. Or, to put it in negative terms, if a minimum level of contentment is not achieved, our spirit or mood is going to depend entirely on our circumstances, both good and bad, and life then becomes an emotional roller coaster with abrupt changes from euphoria to the deepest darkness. It is like a car with worn-out shock absorbers. The tiniest bump becomes a terrific jolt. Many people travel through life without any 'shock absorbers' because they have not learned what contentment means. The secret of contentment, therefore, lies in achieving a certain degree of 'independence' from significant events and not being trapped by them.

How do we achieve this? What must we learn to see differently? Our learning occurs on two levels: on the one hand, horizontally, where we must have a correct understanding of the thorn; and also vertically, where we need a correct understanding of God in the midst of the suffering. Let's examine these two levels in three specific proposals:

Seeing the thorn from the proper perspective

This involves finding the correct distance between what is happening to us and how it affects us. The key word here is *distance*, because distance is what gives us a more objective and global view. Two illustrations will help. If I am lost in a forest, the best way to find the way out is to seek a higher spot from which I will be able to view the situation from a different perspective. The deeper I go into the forest, the harder it will be to find the way out. What is the equivalent to going deeper into a forest and searching unsuccessfully for the exit? *Introspection*. Introspection is, in simple terms, like salt in cooking: a small amount is advisable because it helps us to listen to our inner voice and develop our ability to reflect. Ultimately this facilitates the assimilation of the thorn, something highly desirable. But to poke and dig around all the time inside ourselves leads us into a maze of sensations and distressing feelings. From an excess of introspection usually come endless 'whys'. This ability to 'climb up' to the highest point is what is expressed by the word *surmount* (from Old French *surmonter*: to rise above, go beyond; *sur* 'beyond' + *monter* 'to go up'). When I leave the forest and look for a higher point, I am *surmounting*. To surmount a problem is not so much to solve it as to be able to look upon it 'from on high'. This new perspective is the first step in experiencing peace and calm in the middle of the storm.

The other illustration takes us to a museum. If I want to see a painting correctly, I must find the right distance: if I am too close I will be able to see small isolated fragments quite well, but unable to see the whole picture, and therefore unable to understand the content. Something similar can happen with the experience of the thorn: when the person is engulfed by the problem they are unable to understand anything because they are able to see only small fragments of the situation, thereby missing the whole.

Seeing what is essential over what is circumstantial
The second dimension is the result of the previous one. When I am able to climb up to a vantage point and view the thorn from a correct distance, my eyes open to a panoramic view of life in its entirety. The horizon is wider, and the past and the future take on a different meaning because I am no longer enclosed in a present that is oppressive to the point of crushing me. I discover that the landscape is much more varied and richer than it seemed. Above all, this helps me to rediscover true values and what is essential. I see that the thorn can take away major parts of my life, but the part that remains is still greater. This gives the freedom to react like that tetraplegic journalist and say, 'Yes, I have lost something, but I'm still a millionaire.'

Glimpsing God beyond the thorn
The third reality that I discover in contentment, as I acquire this new and broader vision, is the presence of a God who at first seemed distant, sometimes so distant that I could even mistake him for a ghost, as once happened to the disciples. When on that dark, stormy night on the Sea of Galilee Jesus came to them, walking on the water, they thought he was a phantom. Jesus was with them, and was on their side, but anxiety prevented them from perceiving reality. So great was their anguish, so prolonged their suffering, after rowing all night in adverse conditions, that their ability to perceive and interpret reality correctly was blunted.

And this is often what happens in the early stages of suffering from a thorn. But little by little I learn to *see* that God is not as far away as I thought, nor a mysterious ghost. Rather, he is the suffering Jesus who comes walking towards me, speaking words of encouragement and taking me firmly by the hand so that I don't sink.

Not mistaking God for a ghost and being able to hear his voice in the midst of the thorn is probably the most difficult aspect of acceptance, which is why I will devote the next chapter entirely to this subject. Suffice it to say that being able to see God beyond the thorn produces a trust that is serene and deep. If God is not a distant ghost but the nearby Christ who has suffered much more than I have, then I can learn that nothing occurs in my life without his knowledge and control. If he sees and knows my situation, then I should look at it from the divine point of view as much as is possible. This will enable me to move from a narrow field of vision to a broader horizon, a new 'landscape', as seen from God's perspective, gradually freeing me from bitterness, resentment and feelings of injustice and barrenness. It goes even further: acceptance implies believing that God can bring forth good from any situation, transforming it for his glory.

This ability to see God beyond the thorn is brilliantly summarized in the words of the patriarch Joseph, when he exclaimed before his brothers: 'You intended to harm me, but God meant it for good' (Genesis 50:20). Contentment is inseparable from confidence in a personal God who directs each step of my life with meaning and purpose.

Contentment is a long course, not a quick lesson

If contentment means looking at life from a divine perspective, it is going to take time. As we live in an instant society, where you can get almost everything without having to wait, some people expect to learn contentment quickly. This is a mistake. 'God's University' doesn't hold accelerated courses. Eventually God will give you 'new glasses' so that you may be able to see the thorn differently, but, as in all learning, the process will be extended, with ups and downs and failures on the part of the learner (see chapter 5). There is no doubt that it took a long time for Paul to learn to live with contentment. He himself uses two different verbs in this passage that refer to the learning process: 'I have learned' (v. 11) and 'I am instructed' – or 'initiated' – (v. 12). In both instances the idea is that his learning was not the result of a specific and unique experience, something fast and miraculous; rather, it was a long process requiring many 'classes' in repeated personal encounters with the Lord.

But what is the key to being able to see differently and thus react like the apostle? This takes us to the second subject that we must pass in the difficult course of acceptance: learning to *think* differently.

Learning to think differently: as you think, so you feel

... we take captive every thought to make it obedient to Christ
(2 Corinthians 10:5b).

'Little by little, I felt much better. I wondered why, since the circumstances were the same. Nothing had changed. Then, as if my eyes had been suddenly opened, I realized that it was *me* who had changed.' These words, from a young man who lost an arm in a road accident, remind us of a basic principle: we cannot always change the circumstances, but we can indeed always change *our attitude* towards these circumstances. But how?

In order to see differently we need to learn to *think* differently. As we saw earlier, these two occur simultaneously, not consecutively. The vital principle here is: how we feel depends to a great extent on how we think. The important thing is not what's happening to us but how we interpret what is happening to us. In other words, *you cannot control the events of your life, but you can decide how much they affect you.* Once we are able to understand and accept this, we can start to master our emotions much better than we had imagined. It is important that I explain in detail why this is vital for the process of accepting the thorn.

Planting the right seeds, watering the right plants

First, let's take a look at the psychological mechanism. Thoughts come to us before emotions and are basically what make us feel good or bad, fortunate or unfortunate. My feelings are greatly determined by how I think. My personality is like a garden in which I am constantly planting seeds – my thoughts. The seeds I sow will determine what plants will grow. If it's an encouraging thought, it will make me feel good. If I sow discouraging or pessimistic ideas, I will reap anxiety or depressive feelings. Even without realizing it, I am continually sending messages to my brain that will greatly influence my state of mind, my quality of life and even my health. You might object, 'But, what about the seeds that I did not plant, which just happened to grow in my garden?' Even in these likely cases, there is something you can do: you can water them or just let them go dry and wither. In other words, you cannot choose what plants (thoughts) grow in your garden, but you can certainly choose which ones you water. Martin Luther, leading light of the Reformation, used another illustration: 'You cannot stop birds flying over your head, but you can indeed prevent them from making their nests in your hair.'

Therefore, if our thoughts are largely responsible for our emotions, the consequence is obvious: to be happy or miserable depends, to a great extent, on how we react to adversity. So here we find the main reason why people react differently when facing the same incident: they interpret it differently. Consider this case: 'I can't take it any longer; it's making me bitter and, besides, it's going to last for ever.' These words, spoken by a middle-aged man with diabetes, which affected his eyesight and prevented him from carrying out his regular activities, reflect his negative feelings towards the thorn. I remember another man in a very similar situation, who interpreted his significant limitations as a great opportunity to do certain things in life that he could never have done otherwise: enjoying his grandchildren, developing a helping or counselling ministry by phone, and enriching his relationship with God by praying. The former interpreted his situation as a source of frustration and felt irritated. The latter discovered in his thorn an open door to unexpected opportunities.

Notice that these two men counted on the same powerful tool, their brain, which could work in their favour as an ally, or against them as an enemy. Choosing one or the other will have a decisive influence on my acceptance (or otherwise) of the thorn. Therefore, a key part of the acceptance process lies in *a decision that I make, not in the adverse event* that is 'pummelling' me. In the same way that love implies feelings but ultimately is an act of the will, so it is with acceptance. Therefore, the more we learn to control our thoughts, the more we will control our emotions. As a contemporary psychologist says, 'Attitude is the paintbrush with which the mind colours our life.'[4]

'I am not supposed to feel like this': cognitive therapy in the Bible
This basic principle, i.e. what we feel depends to a great extent on what we think, has produced in psychology what is known as *cognitive therapy*.

This consists of substituting negative or distorted thoughts, called false beliefs, with positive thoughts, which are adapted to reality and generate positive emotions. This process of 'relearning how to think' is similar to the process of studying a foreign language: it must be practised, it requires will power, and it is not instantaneous. For us, as believers, it is very interesting to discover that cognitive therapy is not an invention of modern psychology but was already taught by the apostle Paul to his readers twenty centuries ago! Two passages stand out in this regard, in 2 Corinthians and in Philippians.

Let's look, first of all, at the text in **2 Corinthians**:

> . . . we take captive every thought to make it obedient to Christ
> (2 Corinthians 10:5b).

Cognitive therapy, according to this text, has two main features:

- It requires effort. The idea of *'taking captive'* implies a prior fight or battle. One must fight negative thoughts, disarm them and make them prisoners or captives. This excludes a passive attitude. We have to make the effort, and this is where the will plays a key role. One of the best allies of pessimism or negative thinking is laziness, the lack of effort that is a breeding ground for the self-pity and bitterness already described.
- Its goal is greater obedience to Christ. The step that comes after dominating and taking captive my negative thoughts is to take them to Christ. Here, the cognitive therapy practised by a Christian is radically different from the humanistic approach. The thought control does not seek only, or primarily, my personal benefit, but has a very specific goal: Christ and obedience to his will. To achieve mental peace is legitimate, as we will see in the next section, but this peace that *'surpasses all understanding'* is not the goal, but rather one of the beneficial effects. There is an ethical dimension that implies change, growth into Christ-likeness, a hallmark of any Christian approach to therapy: *holiness comes before happiness*; the purpose of the disciple's life being primarily to please and obey God, not to feel better with every passing day. For the Christian, the practice of cognitive therapy is ultimately focused on God and not on man. This emphasis delivers us from

the contemporary hedonism that establishes that *my* happiness is the highest goal of all.

The passage in Philippians, which is a summary of cognitive therapy, is a priceless pearl for bringing peace to a believer. It is nearly impossible to come to accept any thorn fully without learning and practising the message contained in this key passage.

> Finally, brothers, whatever is true, whatever is noble, whatever is right, whatever is pure, whatever is lovely, whatever is admirable – if anything is excellent or praiseworthy – think about such things (Philippians 4:8).

Here also two main ideas related to cognitive learning spring from the text:

- The eight qualities in the above list have a clear *moral* connotation. They affect not only my frame of mind or my feelings, but also my behaviour, as we have also seen in the text of Corinthians. The benefit is not only psychological – mental relaxation, an anti-anxiety effect – but also ethical. In the measure that I cultivate, '*think about*', this list of virtues, it will affect not only my mind but also my behaviour and relationships. Once more, we see how much the biblical cognitive therapy is removed from the self-centred and hedonistic approach of the popular self-help trend.
- The verb 'to think' – *logizomai* – does not so much mean 'to have in mind' or 'to remember' as it does, above all, 'to reflect, ponder or weigh the true value of something before applying it to life'. Its positive effect is therefore not fleeting, a brief period of 'transcendental meditation' that helps me to relax; rather, it affects my life in a deep and lasting way; it's a habit that shapes my conduct.

'*A peace that surpasses all understanding*': the ultimate benefit of cognitive therapy

There is a close connection between the practice of this biblical cognitive therapy and peace. It is not by chance that as a majestic opening door to the whole section on contentment we find this golden statement: 'And the peace of God, which transcends all understanding, will guard your hearts and your minds in Christ Jesus' (Philippians 4:7). It is on this solid foundation that Paul starts elaborating his thoughts till verse 13. The apostle teaches us here that:

- The *source* of this peace is God himself. It does not spring from any human resource, but from the personal relationship with him through Christ. An inseparable relationship exists between the peace of God and the God of peace.
- Its cardinal *outcome* is keeping us *'guarded'* – sheltered – in Christ Jesus. The verb used here is a military term referring to soldiers standing at their watch to protect – *'guard'* – a certain place. The peace of God is not so much a feeling as an *existential position.* Paul himself described this position in a wonderful way in Romans 8:35, 39: 'Who shall separate us from the love of Christ? ... For I am convinced that nothing in all creation will be able to separate us from the love of God that is in Christ Jesus our Lord.'
- Its beneficial *effects* reach the whole of our personality: not only the *mind*, but also the *heart* (implying emotions and will) are guarded by such peace. In fact for the Hebrews, *shalom* was complete peace that affects the whole person: mind, body and spirit.

Disarming the negative thoughts: cognitive therapy applied to the thorn
We have already seen the vital necessity of changing paralysing negative attitudes and substituting them for others that will be a source of strength and hope.

Let's identify, first of all, the most frequent **negative thought patterns**. A person afflicted by a thorn tends to believe the following wrong ideas:

- *'It's my fault.'* A *personal* cause is sought for the adversity. To blame oneself is a natural reaction in bereavement, which eventually disappears. If the guilt becomes persistent, it means stagnation in the process of acceptance.
- *'It's never going to change.'* The thorn is going to be *permanent.* There is no light in the future; everything seems dark. The world has come to an end.
- *'It's going to ruin my whole life.'* The effects are *global*, permeating every area. I'm unable to do anything. Life is over for me. There is no hope for the future.

This classical triad of negative thoughts – a personal, global and permanent interpretation – is the best way to destroy our self-esteem and bring about feelings of defeat and powerlessness. They generate reactions like 'What am I going to do now? How am I going to manage to pull myself through this?', which are equally negative and debilitating. A vicious circle is established, ending up in a crippling situation which needs to be changed into a more positive interpretation of reality.

Positive thought patterns and habits

What should we do then? How can we fight against these wrong attitudes? Let's remember the golden rule of cognitive therapy: as we think, so we are; it is not our circumstances but rather our attitudes that make us happy or miserable. This is why we need to learn how to ask *reinforcing* questions that produce positive answers and ultimately feelings of hope. In my experience of counselling I have found four questions very helpful. I am thinking not only about people suffering with a thorn but also about those wanting to help them.

- Can I do something to change or improve my situation? Is there some remedy that will help alleviate it? If so, however small the first step may be, let me take it now. Tiny changes can produce major effects. We must not be too ambitious – 'everything or nothing' – in order to begin to take action.
- What is, or could be, good about this situation? We can discover surprisingly positive aspects in a number of difficult situations. But we must bear in mind that these aspects must be sought out actively; rarely are they to be found by chance. Personally it greatly helps me to remember the situation of gold miners: gold nuggets are always found in mud; there's no gold without sludge. One has to dig through the sludge and grime of the mud in order to find the gold.
- What can I learn – about myself and about others? What does God want to teach me regarding his will for my life? The instructive value of suffering is something accepted not only by believers but also by those who understand the secrets of the human soul: teachers, psychoanalysts and authors, among others.
- Is there something for which, or someone for whom, you can be thankful? Look for reasons to be thankful to God or to others.

Normally, circumstances in which we are suffering are an
excellent opportunity for expressing love and solidarity. One of
humanity's worst natural catastrophes in the past centuries, the
2004 tsunami which claimed 250,000 lives, produced one of the
greatest manifestations of solidarity ever known in history.

We will answer some of these questions more fully in the following
chapters.[5] For now it suffices to say that the answer often does not
appear immediately. Time is needed to discover rays of light in the
darkness around us, as Albert Schweitzer pointed out in the quotation
at the beginning of this book: '... You get to discover, one by one,
thousands of stars where hitherto only darkness could be seen.'

In order to complete the process of looking at these positive habits,
we need to mention two unhealthy attitudes that should be avoided:

- *Avoid 'terriblizing'*. This word, which doesn't appear in the
  dictionary, refers to always imagining the very worst scenario,
  that which is most terrible. I interpret my thorn as an earthquake
  that has left no stone unturned in my life. As we saw earlier, one
  of the most helpful exercises in cognitive therapy consists of
  correctly evaluating the 'damage' inflicted by the traumatic
  experience, its consequences, and also my resources. It's a matter
  of properly establishing the dimensions of the problem.
      Two very favourable consequences result from seeing the
  problem in its true proportions. On the one hand, the reduction
  of the negative emotional reaction (anxiety, bereavement, etc.),
  which always arises from the traumatic shock, and, on the other,
  being enabled to develop possible exits and battle strategies much
  more objectively and wisely. Therefore, the correct interpretation
  of the nature and consequences of the thorn is essential to fight
  and not be paralysed by self-pity. It's possible that the shock of the
  thorn may have affected noble parts of the structure of your life or
  of your family, but it has not caved in completely. What you have
  before you are not ruins, but a life filled with immense possibilities.
- *Avoid chronic moaning and wailing*. A frequent pattern seen in
  distorted thoughts involves focusing the attention on *what I do not
  have, what I cannot do, what I am lacking*, instead of focusing on all
  that I still have. To bemoan what I no longer have prevents me

from enjoying what is still within my reach, which, in the case of most thorns, remains greater than that which has been lost.

When a patient has lost the mobility of an arm or a leg, owing to a stroke or an accident, one of the first lessons in rehabilitation is to get them to see how much they can still do with the other arm or leg, and how other functions, such as the sense organs or the brain, are still working perfectly. When patients come to see me because they are suffering from a thorn, I always recommend a simple practical exercise: make a list with two columns: on the right, the things that they still have and can still do; on the left, the things they have lost, their limitations. The result of this exercise is as surprising as it is illuminating.

So far we have considered the healthy results of practising cognitive therapy from a true biblical perspective. One word of caution, however, is needed. Sometimes this kind of self-help is not enough and some form of professional counselling will be necessary. This is true when there is no progress whatsoever and the process becomes chronic, with the complications described in chapter 2. Therefore, seeking appropriate professional help will be the best solution in certain situations.

The basement and the attic of life: David, an example to be copied

We all have in our minds something like two 'rooms': a cellar and an attic. In the cellar, the lowest floor, there is only darkness, dampness and the odd mouse or two. It's not pleasant to remain there. The attic, on the other hand, is the place that receives the most sunlight in the entire house; it is well ventilated and we enjoy being there. It is in the cellar of our mind that we find all the problems, sadness and worry. It is real; it exists – we all have a cellar. But, thank God, we also have an attic, where we find the reasons for our happiness, for gratitude, for the good things of life, for the big and small things that excite us. Why is it that so many people insist on going down to the cellar so often and staying there for such a long time? Is it so difficult to go up to the attic and fill our mind with light, fresh air and gratitude?

In Psalm 103 we have an extraordinary example of how to go up to the attic of life and review, one by one, the blessings of God. We must remember that David suffered the oppressive experience of a thorn in the form of another person, Saul, who haunted him for years, trying to kill him. David had many reasons to complain to the Lord and bemoan his situation, as in fact he does in some of his psalms. Nevertheless, how illuminating and stimulating are his words here:

> Praise the LORD, O my soul;
>   all my inmost being, praise his holy name.
> Praise the LORD, O my soul,
>   and forget not all his benefits –
> who forgives all your sins
>   and heals all your diseases,
> who redeems your life from the pit
>   and crowns you with love and compassion,
> who satisfies your desires with good things
>   so that your youth is renewed like the eagle's.
> (Psalm 103:1–5)

Observe how the Psalmist, in a spontaneous exercise of cognitive therapy, has a dialogue with himself and sends his mind stimulating and strengthening messages: 'Praise the LORD, O my soul' and 'forget not all his benefits'. In fact, if we take our illustration further, it always requires much less effort to go down than to go up. That's why David begins this prayer of Psalm 103 by making an effort to go up to the attic of his life and discover the innumerable reasons for praise and gratitude to God.

How we all need to learn from David, both those who live in anguish from a thorn and also those who do not. To go up to the attic of our mind, and avoid settling down in the cellar as much as possible, is the best way to be able to exclaim, 'Praise the LORD, O my soul, and forget not all his benefits'. This is an essential step on the road to acceptance.

Learning to live differently: adaptation

> I know both how to be abased, and I know how to abound: every where and in all things I am instructed (Philippians 4:12, KJV).

This third stage is the consequence of the first two 'lessons' in the course of acceptance. There is a logical order in the process: once you have learned to see and think differently about the thorn, you are naturally prepared to live in a different way, to make all the changes necessary to allow you to adapt to the new situation. For this reason, the degree of adaptation will be a good test to measure your progress in the process of acceptance.

Let's return now to Paul's experience to understand how adaptation works in practice. In the passage in Philippians 4, which is our text for the entire topic of acceptance, the apostle, after his solemn declaration in verse 11, 'I have learned to be content whatever the circumstances', mentions specific situations in which he has had to learn (v. 12). Although Paul is alluding here, above all, to his material situation, we know that his life was an excellent example of adaptation to one or several thorns. Let's look in greater detail at three of the 'lessons' that Paul had to learn, each containing a key prerequisite for the process of adaptation:

- Willingness to change: flexibility
- Willingness to learn new 'languages' (skills): perseverance and humility
- Willingness to adapt to the loss of autonomy: trust.

Willingness to change: flexibility and resilience

Walking along a beach in a nature reserve on the Balearic island of Menorca, I noticed how the bushes and trees were heavily bent in one direction. The strong north wind buffeting that part of the island had shaped a landscape in a curious and highly symbolic way. It was spectacular to see the thick trunks of pines bent as if they were rubber toys. Why is it that some trees break when struck by a hurricane, while others adapt to the aggressive force of the wind and bend? The key word is *flexibility*. The more inflexible a tree, or indeed any other object, the greater the danger of its breaking under pressure or strong impacts. On the other hand, the more flexible a tree is, the better it will adapt to severe pressure without breaking.

When facing a thorn, people are just like trees: we have the ability to adapt, enabling us to *resist and reorganize* our lives. This 'elastic' ability is known today as **resilience**: the ability to recover following a trauma experience. An understanding of the original usage of the word shows us the richness of its meaning. The term is applied in two main areas: in metallurgy, it refers to a material's ability to return to its initial condition after suffering a sharp blow. In physics, the word alludes to the resistance of materials to pressure and to regaining their original structure. The French psychiatrist and ethologist Boris Cyrulnik was a pioneer in the introduction of this idea in the field of psychology. He applied it to children who have been victims of major childhood traumas (for example, survivors of Nazi concentration camps). In his thought-provoking works,[6] Cyrulnik shows how an unhappy childhood does not necessarily determine the outcome of a person's life. His concepts are also valid for adults, particularly his emphasis on love as the supreme therapeutic force, as we will consider in chapter 5.

A resilient person is like the trees on the island of Menorca: when buffeted by strong winds, they adapt. There are certainly some personal factors, especially relating to our temperament and our genetic make-up, which will make this process easier for some than for others. But, even allowing for the fact that we are all very different from one another, the basic potential for resilience and adaptation is within every human being.

Inseparable from the idea of flexibility is the willingness to change. Change is an inescapable part of life. In fact, our survival as a race depends to a great extent on our ability to change and adapt to new circumstances. Nevertheless, in most people change produces anxiety, because it sends us into unknown situations. In psychology this is called 'boarding' or 'start-up anxiety', a phenomenon that, to a greater or lesser degree, affects everyone and is therefore quite normal. Flexibility is the tool that helps us to assimilate the changes entailed by every thorn. Inasmuch as it diminishes the stress of change, it becomes an essential instrument in living with the new situation, and thus enables us to fight better.

Lack of flexibility, on the other hand, causes us to remain anchored in the past, yearning for what we once were or had and lamenting, like the Spanish poet J. Manrique, 'that any time past was better'. A rigid or inflexible person does not know how to adapt to the present, fears for the future and takes refuge in the past. Such an attitude is a great hindrance to adaptation.

The apostle Paul was a true master of this willingness to adapt. His dramatic conversion was such a radical change that it affected even the deepest part of his identity, symbolized by a new name. Saul, the persecutor, came to be Paul, the persecuted. From a respectable social position, he came to be a pariah to his former Pharisee colleagues; from enjoying authority, he came to suffer beating and imprisonment. In a memorable passage, Philippians 3:7–8, Paul opens his heart to us to share in detail the enormous transformation that Christ brought into his life:

> But whatever was to my profit I now consider loss for the sake of Christ. What is more, I consider everything a loss compared to the surpassing greatness of knowing Christ Jesus my Lord, for whose sake I have lost all things. I consider them rubbish, that I may gain Christ...

In the same way, in 2 Corinthians he describes his emotional state further, as: 'dying, and yet we live on; beaten, and yet not killed; sorrowful, yet always rejoicing; poor, yet making many rich; having nothing, and yet possessing everything' (2 Corinthians 6:9c–10). Amazing paradoxes that powerfully describe the depth of contentment! There is always a contrast between these two levels of reality: the outward appearance, usually related to feelings, and a deeper condition, usually related to convictions and certainties.

Willingness to learn new 'languages' or skills: perseverance and humility

The second essential device to help us adapt to the unknown world of the thorn is to develop new skills, ways of life that diminish the impact of the thorn. This is somewhat like learning a language we have never spoken before. At times it is literally a new language, as with a person who becomes blind and must study Braille. At other times it is a manual or technical learning process: a physically disabled person learning to move about in a wheelchair. Sometimes it is a new relationship, different from all previous relationships, such as parents who must learn to communicate with a son or daughter who is mentally disabled. The list of examples is endless. Almost every thorn requires a new language.

Again the example of the apostle Paul is challenging. He was so aware of this need to adapt to people and circumstances for the sake of Christ that he even said: 'I have become all things to all men . . .' (1 Corinthians 9:22). He had previously mentioned five situations of adaptation (vv. 19–22), taking it for granted that no powerful witness for Christ can be possible without this strong willingness to 'become all things to all men'.

The common characteristic in the learning of all these languages is that they make us feel like children again. We have to learn how to walk, talk, read and even mix with each other in completely unfamiliar ways.

That's why the fundamental requirement here is double: **humility and perseverance**. At first, the obstacle seems insurmountable. That's normal. Children taking their first steps will fall umpteen times before becoming agile enough to walk with confidence. Adults learning a foreign language feel as limited in their vocabulary as children babbling their first words. It doesn't matter if you feel as if you have returned to infancy. You are starting a new stage in your life in which you are chronologically a child. That's why, far from discouraging you, it should be a source of hope: infancy is naturally followed by adulthood. If you face this learning period with the humility and perseverance of a child, you will soon discover that what at first seemed a problem becomes an opportunity, the opportunity to 'speak' new languages that enrich you and open up new and unexpected perspectives of personal growth.

Willingness to adapt to the loss of autonomy: trust

One of the most painful consequences of some thorns is not being able to manage on one's own. To have to depend on others is probably the most difficult adjustment in the entire process. Personal autonomy is a precious gift that we take for granted until we lose it. Elderly people know this feeling quite well. The words of the Lord Jesus to Peter are so very true: 'I tell you the truth, when you were younger you dressed yourself and went where you wanted; but when you are old you will stretch out your hands, and someone else will dress you and lead you where you do not want to go' (John 21:18).

Nevertheless, we must learn to ask for help. This may seem obvious. Do we really need to learn something so elementary? Yes, certainly, when this question comes from a powerless person who *wants to but cannot*. It is quite a different matter when a person *can but does not want to*. In fact, the thorn generates a degree of inability that forces us to ask for help. And this type of forced dependency is difficult for all of us because it awakens in us feelings of shame and humiliation. To need something from others hurts our self-esteem. Deep down we all have a sense of pride that makes us feel bad when we need to depend on the favour of others. We think that it is only the 'poor', in whatever sense, who must ask for help. This is a mistake that arises from an unbiblical feeling of self-sufficiency. There is no reason why we should feel ashamed or humiliated by asking for help when we need it. Deep down, this is the core of the gospel: 'This poor man called, and the LORD heard him' (Psalm 34:6).

The key requirement here is **trust**. We are not referring here to trust in God, already described in the previous chapter as the basic equipment for the journey. In the struggle against the thorn it is also important to learn to *trust others*. Of course, we do not mean that you should trust just anyone or everyone. It is a matter of establishing a special and solid bond with a few very significant people who become a kind of extension of yourself in a rich, meaningful relationship that was unthinkable without the thorn. In fact, the mysterious strength of this bond is bilateral: caregivers also come to feel this intense sense of love and mutual belonging. I will never forget the impact of seeing the relationship of a young couple, good friends of mine, with their son, who suffered from severe infantile cerebral palsy. What rich non-verbal communication, what affection in their kisses and gentle caresses, and in every word that the child did not seem to understand with his head but did with his heart!

David's relationship with Jonathan is an example of this. Constantly on the run from Saul, in a life-or-death struggle, David established such a strong bond of trust with his bosom friend Jonathan that he came to say in that beautiful elegy: 'Your love for me was wonderful, more wonderful than that of women' (2 Samuel 1:26). And in another passage we read: 'After David had finished talking with Saul, Jonathan became one in spirit with David, and he loved him as himself . . . And Jonathan made a covenant with David because he loved him as himself' (1 Samuel 18:1, 3). Humanly speaking, many times David's life depended on the help and information that Jonathan gave him. Jonathan was instrumental in helping him escape and adapt to so many years of desert experience. Rarely does God abandon us to face the thorn by ourselves. He usually provides a 'Jonathan' who helps us decisively in our battle. What a great privilege!

Paul also had to make this discovery. Sometimes it was the problem with his eyes that forced him to depend on others, for example when writing his epistles, such as the one to the Galatians: 'See what large letters I use as I write to you with my own hand' (Galatians 6:11). At other times it was his imprisonment, the maximum expression of loss of autonomy and freedom; this was the case with the letter to the Philippians, written from the prison in Rome. These situations caused him to be dependent on certain chosen helpers, people he trusted, such as Timothy and others with whom he came to have an extraordinary relationship. Outstanding was the feeling Paul had towards Epaphroditus, richly described in Philippians 2:25–30.

Try to discover your Jonathan or Epaphroditus as you struggle against the thorn. It can become one of the most enriching experiences in life.

Christ, the supreme model of acceptance in the face of the greatest of all thorns

There is a supreme example of acceptance: Christ, who faced the thorn of sin and death on the cross. Can there be an experience more physically and morally traumatic than this? On the cross, Christ endured one of the most sadistic forms of death from a physical point of view[7] and, above all, the greatest injustice and moral pain suffered by anyone ever. It is not by accident that the word *sting* – similar to the thorn with its sharp painful effects – is used to describe death and sin: 'Where, O death, is your victory? Where, O death, is your sting? The sting of death is sin, and the power of sin is the law' (1 Corinthians 15:55–56). Jesus had to suffer the worst of all thorns – death and the weight of sin – precisely to free us from its mortal venom.

Our experiences of pain can be very difficult to bear, but they are put into perspective when contrasted with that thorn above all thorns, the cross. No human thorn can be greater than this: 'But he was pierced for our transgressions, he was crushed for our iniquities; the punishment that brought us peace was upon him, and by his wounds we are healed' (Isaiah 53:5). This vivid prophetic passage introduces Jesus as an expert in suffering, with 'a doctorate in thorns': 'He was despised and rejected by men, a man of sorrows, and familiar with suffering' (v. 3). All this because God 'laid on him the iniquity of us all' (v. 6b). A careful reading of this chapter gives us an impressive description of suffering out of love. And it is here that we start to glimpse the powerful rays of light that the gospel throws on the mystery of unjust suffering.

Personally I find it difficult to read this passage without being deeply moved. The powerful words and music of a hymn by Charles Wesley come to mind:

> And can it be that I should gain
> an interest in the Saviour's blood?

Died He for me, who caused His pain?
   For me, who Him to death pursued?
Amazing love! How can it be
   that Thou, my God, shouldst die for me!

On that night of deep anguish, as we contemplate the Lord Jesus in Gethsemane facing the thorn of his dreadful death, we are greatly challenged by his attitudes. In fact, to consider them will be a sort of summary of the steps mentioned so far, especially in Paul's experience.

- 'Father, if you are willing, take this cup from me' (Luke 22:42). Jesus **fights** to eliminate the thorn. As a man, Jesus has the same reaction as any of us: he tries to avoid going through that trauma; he seeks to change things. This is the legitimate and natural fighting phase that we have already considered.
- 'With loud cries and tears.' A **fervent prayer** to the Father. The author of Hebrews describes to us, in almost crude realism, the emotional intensity of Jesus' struggle in prayer with the Father: 'During the days of Jesus' life on earth, he offered up prayers and petitions with loud cries and tears to the one who could save him from death, and he was heard because of his reverent submission' (Hebrews 5:7). From the gospel story we know that he was 'sorrowful and deeply distressed' (Matthew 26:37, NKJV) and that 'being in anguish, he prayed more earnestly, and his sweat was like drops of blood falling to the ground' (Luke 22:44). In Matthew we read: 'My soul is overwhelmed with sorrow to the point of death' (Matthew 26:38).
- 'Yet not my will, but yours be done' (Luke 22:42). A fully **obedient disposition**: 'Yet not as I will, but as you will' (Matthew 26:39). Jesus' subjection to the will of the Father was complete, from the very beginning of his life on earth. The song that appears in Philippians 2 describes it to us in these words: '... he humbled himself and became obedient to death – even death on a cross!' (Philippians 2:8).

The struggle to change things and fervent prayer to that end must always stay within the framework of submission to God's will, even though this may seem mysterious and dark. At first we are surprised by the affirmation that Jesus 'was heard because of his reverent submission' (Hebrews 5:7). In what sense was he heard? God did not save him from death. Jesus had to go through the bitter experience of the cross. From our human perspective, to be heard by the Father ought to imply an affirmative response to Jesus' petition; that is, freeing him from the cross. But we know this did not happen. God heard him in the sense that he sent an angel to strengthen Jesus (Luke 22:43). In the Luke narrative we see a very clear cause-and-effect relationship between Jesus' petition: 'Father, if you are willing, take this cup from me' (Luke 22:42) and the immediate response from the Father: 'An angel from heaven appeared to him and strengthened him' (v. 43). This is an amazing lesson: God does not always free us from the thorn, but he always gives us the resources needed to fight it.

Christ suffered and admirably overcame the greatest of all thorns. As a result, ' . . . we do not have a high priest who is unable to sympathise with our weaknesses, but we have one who has been tempted in every way, just as we are – yet was without sin' (Hebrews 4:15). His victory on the cross provides us with his supernatural grace that strengthens us in our weakness. This is why the author of Hebrews encourages us to 'approach the throne of grace with confidence, so that we may receive mercy and find grace to help us in our time of need' (4:16). Let us approach, then, to obtain this grace of Christ, the supernatural ingredient of acceptance.

4 'When I am weak, then I am strong': God's grace and the strength of weakness

To accept does not mean to indulge in suffering, nor to endure it with fatalism, nor to become hardened from painful trials ... nor to try and forget it with time. It is to offer it to God so He can make it bear fruit. For this reason it is neither reasoned, nor invented, nor understood: it is a spiritual experience.[1]

The change in Paul is surprising: from a man constantly struggling, pleading intensely with God to remove his thorn, he makes an about-turn and affirms with complete conviction, 'I will boast all the more gladly about my weaknesses' (2 Corinthians 12:9). How did he undergo such a complete transformation? The quote from Paul Tournier gives us the clue: 'it is a spiritual experience'. We saw earlier how acceptance could ultimately be achieved only by the grace of God. We call this the *supernatural* ingredient in the process of acceptance: it depends on faith and is not obtained by any other technical means, but through a personal encounter with the God of the Bible. In order to *surmount* the thorn, in addition to the valuable therapeutic resources that science offers us, we must discover and experience this supernatural strength that transforms weaknesses into strengths.

This takes us back to the text in 2 Corinthians 12:7–10, where we find the keys that transformed the apostle Paul so profoundly that he was able to exclaim, 'For when I am weak, then I am strong' (v. 10). It was through permanent fellowship with his Lord that Paul received the ingredient that was decisive in his acceptance of the thorn: grace. Let us consider, first of all, God's answer.

God's answer

My grace is sufficient for you, for my power is made perfect in weakness (2 Corinthians 12:9).

Several times Paul asks the Lord to remove the thorn from him. The answer to this fervent prayer is not liberation but provision of what is *necessary to live with joy* in the midst of his chronic suffering. God does not take away, but gives! We must emphasize this principle because it is fundamental for understanding how God sees our thorn. For us the 'solution' consists in eliminating the problem. God's vision, however, is very different: what is most important is not the absence of suffering but rather his presence in the midst of suffering and the resources his presence affords us. What are these resources?

The answer is found in two words, each alluding to their respective resources for accepting the thorn: *grace* and *power*. Actually, they are intimately related because power – or strength – is the result of grace. Note the emphasis of the text on the *divine origin* of both resources. What in English appears as a simple possessive adjective, 'my', in the original is in the genitive which translates literally as 'the power of me' and 'the grace of me', a grammatical structure that seeks to underline its ownership. This emphasis confirms our point: there are resources that transcend a person's ability or capability and go far beyond any psychological technique or social measure. These resources come from God and can be obtained only through a spiritual experience.

Grace: 'My grace is sufficient for you'
We have before us one of the most wonderful declarations in the entire Bible. This statement, as brief as it is powerful, has been a source of comfort to thousands of believers dealing with weaknesses and trials. Here we find the heart of the struggle against the thorn. This was the

fundamental lesson that Paul needed to learn. The word 'grace' rises majestically in the middle of the passage like a climax. We are reaching the peak of the mountain. The road we have travelled up to this point has been long, sometimes torturous and arduous. Now we have before our eyes the end of the road: *'my grace'*, this grace that is not a cold theological concept but rather the power of God operating in very specific ways in a person and in their circumstances. Grace takes us before the very majesty of God, because, as Thomas Aquinas wrote in his main work *Summa Theologica*, 'grace is nothing else but a certain beginning of glory in us'.

It is worth asking why God answers Paul in such a brief way. What can six words do in the face of so many years of inner struggle and unexplainable suffering? It seems legitimate to infer that God, with his emphatic brevity, wants to make it clear that there is *only one way* to the final victory over the thorn. We can paraphrase what Jesus said to Martha and apply it to grace: 'You are very worried and upset about the thorn, but only one thing is needed. My grace is sufficient for you.'

So what does this expression 'my grace is sufficient for you' mean? And, especially, how does it affect our acceptance of the thorn? As some commentators point out, Calvin among them, the word *grace* alludes to the constant *aid* of the Holy Spirit, which comes to us from the unmerited favour of God. Therefore, not only have we the wonderful gift of God that one day saved us, the saving grace, but also the immense wealth of practical help that he supplies us with every day. *Grace is the sum of supernatural resources that come freely from God and enable us to battle against the thorn with divine power.* The essential difference between a believing and a non-believing person as they face the thorn lies precisely here: in their resources. The suffering can be the same for both, but the believer has certain assets that are not available to the person who does not have a personal faith in God. Later we will consider the valuable components that grace contains.

In what sense is grace *sufficient*? Paul receives just the amount he needs for his acceptance to be 'all the more gladly' (v. 9) and to 'delight in' (v. 10). It's not a matter of merely enduring the thorn or of surviving in the midst of the trial. Such an attitude *is not sufficient*. It's not good when we accept thorns reluctantly, just because we have no other choice. God does not want this kind of forced acceptance, which is closer to stoic resignation. The level of sufficiency that God asks of us is much higher. He doesn't want 'grouchy' children but children who are, in Paul's memorable expression, 'more than conquerors' (Romans 8:37).

Power: 'For my power is made perfect in weakness'

The second sentence begins with 'for', in the sense of 'because', and is an explanation that expands the previous claim. Paul, the man who had previously been transformed by divine grace in a number of facets of his life, probably did not need this explanation, but we do! The Lord does not simply tell Paul to be content with his grace, as if it were an order. The phrase is not imperative, as in 'I order you to . . .' God is not an authoritarian despot. Like a father who seeks not only to console but also to convince, he offers Paul a powerful reason. When struggling with a thorn, a person needs explanations that are indispensable for genuine acceptance. That is why the exhortation is accompanied by a convincing explanation: 'my power is made perfect in weakness'. Here is the secret that helps us understand why God's grace was sufficient. No wonder this passage has become a permanent source of inspiration to all of us who suffer from a thorn.

The great paradox: 'when I am weak, then I am strong' (v. 10)

Logically, a weakness is an obstacle and a limitation. This was how Paul understood his thorn. The lesson that the apostle must now learn is that God's way of thinking is completely different from ours. It is not that Paul's thorn does not bother the Almighty, but that right there – in the weakness – is where the Lord can show his power. And, what's more, it is even perfected in weakness. This is why Paul goes on to affirm: 'Therefore I will boast all the more gladly about my weaknesses, so that Christ's power may rest on me' (2 Corinthians 12:9).

An illustration that Jesus used helps us to understand this paradox. He said of himself, 'I am the light of the world . . . the light shines in the darkness' (John 8:12; 1:5). The light of Christ can shine much more brightly during moments of darkness. It is in the 'dark night of the soul', an expression used by John of the Cross and other Spanish mystics, that we begin to understand this great paradox: in the dark tunnel of my thorn – when I am weak – the light of Christ shines brightest because nothing is camouflaging it. It is then that I am strong because the greater the darkness, the brighter the radiance of his light.

This points to a transcendental matter that goes far beyond the problem of the thorn. It contains a vital principle regarding the relationship between a person and their Creator. A huge obstacle in approaching God is feeling strong, or self-sufficient. Fantasies of omnipotence – the desire to be like God – have been a constant in the history of humankind ever since Adam and Eve were tempted and fell into this sin of self-sufficiency. Pride, one of the main sources of our rebellion against God, becomes a great hindrance to faith. Why? Because it tends to become accentuated when things are going well for us, making us feel 'very important'. If you believe you are like a demigod, there is no place for the real God in your heart. On the other hand, the feeling of weakness, whether physical, moral or existential, tends to be fertile ground for faith in God and for his power to be made manifest.

Of course, it is not always like this. We find notable atheists who suffered greatly, such as Nietzsche, who was tormented by the lacerating thorn of a dreadful disease that led to his insanity. But, many times, behind the utterance of the words 'I don't need God' hides the sin of the church in Laodicea: pride. 'You say, "I am rich; I have acquired wealth and do not need a thing." But you do not realize that you are wretched, pitiful, poor, blind and naked' (Revelation 3:17).

Are we then to conclude that faith is only for weaklings? Or, following Nietzsche's idea, does one have to be sufficiently sick to become a Christian? An exploration of this topic goes beyond the purpose of this book, so I can touch on it only briefly. If we understand 'weak' to mean people of low intellectual capacity or ability, then the answer is clearly 'no'. There are shining examples in God's Word and in history of men and women with privileged minds, noteworthy and brilliant leaders in all areas of human knowledge, who had a deep faith in God. But, in another sense, 'yes'. Faith is for the weak, for those who feel they are 'poor' – as in the first of the beatitudes – when they consider their smallness and their worthlessness in the face of God's greatness and holiness. Jesus himself makes it fully clear to us when he says, 'It is not the healthy who need a doctor, but the sick. I have not come to call the righteous, but sinners to repentance' (Luke 5:31–32). Who are the weak to whom the gospel is directed? Those who realize they are *sinners*. This kind of moral and existential weakness is the exact opposite of pride and self-sufficiency: it is the humility that Paul had to learn precisely through the experience of the thorn. The purpose of the thorn was to prevent arrogance, 'to keep me from becoming conceited because of these surpassingly great revelations' (v. 7).

How does grace operate in reality? In the following chapters we will consider the manifold treasures of grace in relation to the thorn experience, from new strength to a new set of values that give us a new reason to live.

Grace in action: the therapeutic effects of grace

> ... in order that ... he might show the incomparable riches of his grace, expressed in his kindness to us in Christ Jesus (Ephesians 2:7).

Some people claim that they don't need God because, if they're badly off, he'll only make them feel worse. How does one come to think like that? It is very difficult to understand the message of the gospel if God's grace is not properly understood. Therefore, within the ranks of atheism are a multitude of people who rejected God without really knowing him. Among the most convinced atheists, we frequently find experiences based on a God who is severe and merciless. This leads to a legalistic and crushing gospel that ends up being rejected. A well-known example is the Swedish film-maker Ingmar Bergman. When he was a child, the rigid and severe faith of his father had a negative influence on Bergman, leading him eventually to a religious and existential crisis which appeared constantly in his films. The God of the Bible is the 'God of all grace' (1 Peter 5:10), and the heart of the gospel – its deepest essence – is found in grace. When you do not understand this basic reality, faith becomes a burden.

The whole gospel is about grace. For example: the greeting used at the beginning of many epistles is quite significant: 'Grace and peace be unto you from our Lord Jesus Christ.' Grace and peace are the two words that summarize the entire gospel. There is no better summary of the Christian faith. There is a cause-and-effect relationship between the two words: the ultimate source of peace is found in understanding and applying divine grace. Grace leads to peace. And it is here that we start to understand that the wounds of any thorn need the healing effect of the grace and peace of Jesus Christ.

So what *is* grace, for that matter? We can compare it to a treasure containing several precious stones – the *riches* of which Paul speaks. The best-known is salvation: 'For it is by grace you have been saved, through faith – and this not from yourselves, it is the gift of God' (Ephesians 2:8). Above all, grace saves us. This saving effect of grace has become the main pillar of the evangelical creed, as the sixteenth-century Reformation reminds us with its emphasis on *sola gratia*. The forgiveness of sins and the justification in Christ (Romans 5:1) that frees us from eternal condemnation is the first precious stone of grace.

But the effects of grace do not end with salvation. Grace is not only a thing of the past, but continues to manifest itself every day in the life of the believer. We could say that we live 'wrapped' in grace. Therefore we were first saved *by* grace, but we live *under, in, by* grace (the list of prepositions could continue!). Sometimes we give so much emphasis to salvation by grace that we forget about **life by grace**.

Let us now consider three of the main soothing effects of grace when living with a thorn:

- renewed strength: grace empowers
- change: grace transforms
- maturity: grace teaches.

Renewed strength: grace empowers

So that Christ's power may rest on me . . . (2 Corinthians 12:9).

I can do everything through him who gives me strength (Philippians 4:13).

The first therapeutic effect of grace is the renewal of our strength. In a broad sense, grace equips us with God's power so that we can live morally righteous lives. This divine empowering is essential in enabling us to behave on a par with the demands of the gospel. We cannot aspire 'to be holy' by our own strength. Humanly speaking, the Christian life is not difficult – it's impossible! This is why we have to turn to this grace that enables us daily to live in a manner pleasing to God. Paul himself reminds us of our dependency on God: 'For it is God who works in you to will and to act according to His good purpose' (Philippians 2:13).

In a more specific sense, grace strengthens us in our inabilities, weaknesses or suffering. It is in this context that it appears closely related to the word 'power' in 2 Corinthians 12:9–10. In order to better understand how our strength is renewed, let us return to the text of Philippians 4:13: 'I can do everything through him who gives me strength.' The word 'strength' in the original comes from the same word, *dynamis*, that in 2 Corinthians 12 is translated as 'power'. It alludes to an enormous power, not just any power – the word 'dynamite' is derived from it.

What does this sentence really mean? If we do not understand it properly it can be more a source of frustration than a blessing. On the other hand, a complete understanding of its wealth is the key to accepting our thorn. The idea of the text is that when I am *in Christ I can triumph over – I can be stronger than – any situation because he strengthens me*. As some versions correctly translate, in Christ we find 'the strength to face anything'. Note that the verb 'to do' does not occur in the text. The emphasis is not on action but on attitude, an attitude of victory. Paul is not saying that in Christ we can *do* everything that we propose. Being in Christ does not turn us into demigods. As Christians we sometimes harbour 'Superman' fantasies and believe that we have unlimited abilities. This verse is a declaration of sure victory in Christ. It is the attitude of trust and courage that challenges the enemy, in this case the thorn, with the certainty of triumph. It is a serious warning against defeatism.

We find a similar idea in Romans 8:28–39, one of the most light-bearing of texts for someone travelling down the dark tunnel of a thorn. Towards the end of this hymn of unshakeable trust, and after mentioning a long list of thorns, Paul affirms: ' . . . in all these things we are **more than conquerors** through him who loved us'. But in what sense are we *more than conquerors*? This introduces us to the second therapeutic effect of grace.

Change: grace transforms

Therefore I will boast all the more gladly about my weaknesses . . .

The therapeutic effects of grace are progressive and interdependent. The new strength gives way to a profound change that would be impossible were it not for this prior fortitude. In other words, the renewed strength is the foundation upon which a new structure is now going to be built. Here also we will look firstly at a more general aspect of change, and see later how it applies specifically to the thorn. The believer is continuously experiencing an inner transformation that moulds him or her into the image of Christ. The word used in the original is *metamorphoumetha* (2 Corinthians 3:18), and its purpose focuses on our becoming more and more like him every day. This process is very similar to the ripening of fruit or the growth of a child. In fact, the word 'mature' or 'perfect' – *teleios* – appears numerous times in this context of transformation. It is the same word that we find in Philippians 1:6: 'being confident of this, that he who began a good work in you will carry it on to completion until the day of Christ Jesus'. It is in this general sense that Paul affirms: 'by the grace of God I am what I am, and his grace to me was not without effect' (1 Corinthians 15:10). The apostle's transformation, which changed him from 'persecutor' to 'persecuted' (vv. 8–9), is a tremendous example of the transforming power of grace.

What effects does this transforming grace have on the thorn? This same aspect of maturing or growth appears in the phrase 'my power is **perfected** in weakness' (2 Corinthians 12:9). Let us notice, first of all, the conjunction 'therefore'. It is the link that joins God's key answer, in the first part of verse 10, to Paul's reaction. In other words, there is a clear cause-and-effect relationship between the answer from the Lord and the consequences experienced. When God speaks to the heart, something changes.

God can change the circumstances, and certainly this does at times happen. But, above all, God changes people. And when this occurs, even the very same circumstances seem different, as if we are seeing a totally different landscape. That was Paul's experience. His thorn continued as it always had: the same pain, the same humiliation. But something had changed in an extraordinary way. In verse 10 the apostle does not seem to be the same person writing in verse 7. What has happened? Grace, this multifaceted treasure of divine resources, has produced in Paul a transformation of attitudes.

In the previous chapter we considered acceptance more from a psychological angle. Now we will take a closer look at how this change is produced from a spiritual angle. Three main changes guided by the Holy Spirit make a profound spiritual experience:

- the perspective changes: God's binoculars
- attitudes change: the thorn loses its sting
- the situation itself changes: God opens up paths in the desert.

The perspective changes: God's binoculars

> So that the strength and power of Christ may pitch a tent over and dwell upon me (v. 9, Amplified Bible).

God does not remove the thorn from Paul, but he does take away his negative thoughts about it. Remember the main purpose of cognitive therapy is to learn to think positively, and the first step in this process consists of identifying and replacing the negative thoughts with positive ones. The next step – sowing positive thoughts – now appears clearly in the text. Actually, a single thought was enough: 'My power is made perfect in weakness.' The Lord dealt with Paul like a perfect psychologist.

Once this seed is growing in his mind, Paul is able to assimilate the idea and make it his with conviction. Something decisive occurs which is the key to accepting the thorn: *he changes his perspective*. It is as if the Lord gave him new glasses or, better still, a pair of binoculars. Paul sees the same reality but from a totally new perspective; the new lens has increased his field of vision to limits that were previously inaccessible. Now he sees what God sees; his view of the thorn approaches God's.

What does he see now? Let us imagine the following dialogue between the apostle and the Lord: 'Paul, what you consider a hindrance is actually a useful instrument in my hands.'

'In what way, Lord? That's hard for me to understand.'

'The thorn is an opportunity for my power to rest upon you. What you see as a curse is in reality a blessing. I can use something bad for good.'

In essence, a **self-centred lens** is replaced by a **Christ-centred lens**. Before, when Paul looked at his thorn, he saw a poor man buffeted by suffering, an unjust and undeserved situation. He felt wretched and maybe even forgotten by his Lord, a vision that arises from introspection. Now, every time he suffers the scourges of the thorn, he sees Christ and his power *'resting'* upon him. One translation renders the same idea in a more poetic way: 'So that the strength and power of Christ may pitch a tent over and dwell upon me' (Amplified Bible). What a refreshing panorama in the midst of the dryness of the thorn. It is the difference between looking at the 'basement' of life or lifting my eyes to the heights where God is.

Attitudes change: the thorn loses its sting

> That is why ... I delight in weaknesses, in insults, in hardships, in persecutions (v. 10).

Naturally, this change of lens produces a change in attitude. We must not forget that it all springs from the bedrock of renewed strength. Continuing with the imaginary dialogue, Paul now says, 'Lord, this is marvellous; I had never thought about how different everything was for you. Now I discover that my weaknesses become your opportunities. If this is the way it is, I will *very happily* bear this problem. Not only will I not complain but *I will also rejoice* because I know that my limitations are the window through which the splendour of your power shines.'

We discover at least three attitudes that have changed in Paul:

Joy instead of complaint: 'That is why, for Christ's sake, I delight in weaknesses...' (v. 10). Remember that joy is much deeper than a feeling. It is the serene conviction that 'in all these things we are more than conquerors' because no one and nothing 'will be able to separate us from the love of God that is in Christ Jesus our Lord' (Romans 8:37–39).

Voluntary **submission** instead of defiance: 'Therefore I will boast all the more gladly about my weaknesses' (v. 9). His struggle to get rid of the thorn gives way to full submission to the 'cup' of suffering that the Lord allows in his life.

Worship instead of self-pity. Even though worship does not appear explicitly in the text, it is implicit in the attitudes of the apostle that glorify God. Worship and praise in a believer's life are not restricted to special moments but are inseparable from his or her entire behaviour; they are not primarily *activities* but *attitudes*.

With these new attitudes, Paul shows us that although the thorn still buffets him from time to time, it has lost its sting. Because the thorn's greatest danger lies not in the physical pain it may cause, or even in its emotional disturbances, but in the way it poisons attitudes, for then you focus on self-pity, defiance and bitterness. The persistence of such attitudes ultimately 'kills' any desire to live. This is why for God it is much more important to eliminate these attitudes than to remove the thorn itself. Paul has come out triumphant because he has eliminated the sting of his thorn.

The situation changes: God opens up a way in the desert

> See, I am doing a new thing!
>   Now it springs up . . .
> I am making a way in the desert
>   and streams in the wasteland.
> (Isaiah 43:19)

We have seen how grace transforms people. But grace goes even further than that; it can change situations and circumstances. We are not referring here to the normal adaptation that occurs at the end of the adjustment period, but to supernatural changes brought about by the power of God through his grace.

The metaphor of the desert and the wasteland that God uses in Isaiah to give his people hope for a different future has some relevance here. The thorn can continue for many years, sometimes throughout our life, as in the case of Paul. But in the midst of this drought and barrenness, God provides refreshing oases – 'a way in the desert and streams in loneliness' – that renew our strength and enable us to continue. In the first part of the verse (Isaiah 43:19), the expression 'I am doing a new thing' literally means 'a new shoot', like a tree that, in the spring, produces tender new roots, full of life after a long and gruelling winter. The harsh winter is followed by an outburst of new life in the spring, with excitement and new strength. With this double metaphor, God communicates to his people a solid hope for a different future. This can also be the experience of the person afflicted by a thorn when he or she experiences transforming grace.

What are these roads in the desert and the waters in a sterile land? I will mention two of them: the roads that lead us to discover the other side of pain and find specific ways out of the trial, illustrated by the striking example of Joseph in Genesis.

Discovering the other side of pain

One of the most outstanding – and healing – effects of contemplating the thorn from God's perspective is discovering the 'other side' of suffering. Up to this point, Paul has known only an entirely negative side of the thorn: it hurts; it humiliates, 'it buffets me' (NKJV). It is what we would call *the evil of pain*. The other side of the coin is *the good in pain.* The preposition here is very important: we are not saying the good *of* pain but rather the good *in* pain. Suffering in itself is always something undesirable, and we must not make the mistake of 'glorifying' it.

As John Stott says, 'we cannot thank God for absolutely everything, including blatant evil. The strange notion is gaining popularity in some Christian circles that the major secret of Christian freedom and victory is unconditional praise ... and that even the most appalling calamities of life should become subjects for thanksgiving and praise ... God abominates evil, and we cannot praise or thank him for what he abominates.'[2] In fact, to give thanks to God for circumstances of suffering can border on blasphemy. There is an important difference between 'giving thanks *for*' and 'giving thanks *in the midst of*'. In all the epistles we are exhorted to give thanks *in* everything – for example, in 1 Thessalonians 5:18. The only time in which the phrase 'always giving thanks to God the Father *for* everything' (Ephesians 5:20) appears, it is immediately conditioned by the expression 'in the name of our Lord Jesus Christ'. In other words, it must be consistent with the nature and will of Christ himself.

Therefore, I am to maintain an attitude of gratitude and praise in the midst of the pain caused by this thorn. This is exactly what David did in numerous psalms written in his literal desert – when he hid there, fleeing from Saul, his 'thorn' – as well as in his metaphorical desert – the many years of apparently sterile life. One example is Psalm 57, written when David escaped from Saul to the cave of Adullam. In verse 4 he describes his deep anguish: 'I am in the midst of lions; I lie among ravenous beasts – men whose teeth are spears and arrows, whose tongues are sharp swords.' But in the midst of these circumstances – death threats – he bursts out in a serene exclamation of praise that becomes a beautiful hymn of trust:

Be exalted, O God, above the heavens;
    let your glory be over all the earth.

They spread a net for my feet –
    I was bowed down in distress.
They dug a pit in my path –
    but they have fallen into it themselves.

My heart is steadfast, O God,
  my heart is steadfast;
  I will sing and make music.
Awake, my soul!
  Awake, harp and lyre!
  I will awaken the dawn.

I will praise you, O Lord, among the nations;
  I will sing of you among the peoples.
For great is your love, reaching to the heavens;
  your faithfulness reaches to the skies.

Be exalted, O God, above the heavens;
  let your glory be over all the earth.
(Psalm 57:5–11)

To discover this other side of suffering is to experience that 'in all things God works for the good of those who love him' (Romans 8:28). Here we are touching on one of the most mysterious aspects of grace: at the same time something glorious and difficult to understand. We are standing on 'holy ground', which we approach both with reverence and with perplexity, like Moses on Mount Horeb. Paul does not leave any room for doubt and affirms categorically, 'In **all** things God works for the good.' This includes, therefore, every thorn and any type of trial, as he himself explains in the exhaustive list in verse 35. In a mysterious and paradoxical way, suffering becomes an instrument to fulfil some specific purposes for our lives.

Becoming aware of this 'way in the desert' – the good in pain – can take time, sometimes a very long time. It is part of the maturity process described earlier, operated by grace, and it does not come about by mere introspection. But when it is achieved, it produces a revolutionary change in the way I face the thorn. I shall never forget the words spoken by the parents of a Down's syndrome child: 'At the beginning our world came crashing down on us, but our child has been like an angel to us, an angel sent by God. Before, we were always arguing and there was tension in our marriage. Since our child was born, his sweetness and affection make all that impossible.'

Finding the way out, not instant solutions

The roads in the desert and the water in the parched land are not just a matter of discovering the good in the evil, a difficult and sometimes long-term task. There is another way by which God provides relief to the pilgrim overwhelmed by the thorn: his *active* intervention can change the circumstances by providing specific ways out. Actually, this is a promise for every Christian in every tribulation. Such is the underlying principle of 1 Corinthians 10:13: 'God is faithful; he will not let you be tempted beyond what you can bear. But when you are tempted, he will also provide a way out so that you can stand up under it.'

God provides *a way out* – not *a solution*. A solution is something that occurs instantly, almost magically, eliminating the problem automatically. This is what many people expect today in a hedonistic society where suffering is scarcely tolerated and is considered a troublesome distraction. We want solutions, and we want them 'now'. It is interesting to note that the word 'solution' does not occur at all in the Bible. A 'way out', on the other hand, is a door that opens onto a road that must be walked. Remember, for example, how in Isaiah 43 what God provides is precisely *a way*. Herein lies the great difference: a solution does not require any effort at all – the thorn simply disappears; on the other hand, in providing a way out, God shows us the road we must walk along. Of course, this road is not always easy. The way out that he gave the people of Israel from the thorn of the tyranny of Pharaoh entailed forty years in the desert!

The Bible contains beautiful examples of this transformation of circumstances, carried out by grace in the midst of *thorny* situations. Let us consider one of the most noteworthy examples: Joseph, the patriarch, considered an archetype of Christ and, therefore, a valuable model for us.

Transforming tragedies into 'fables': Joseph's life, a monument to God's providence

> You intended to harm me, but God intended it for good (Genesis 50:20).

I remember an interview with the Argentinian author Jorge L. Borges in which he said, 'Kafka's mastery consisted in his ability to transform tragedies into fables.' Since a fable is a literary composition with a useful or moral teaching, a thought immediately came to mind: my God is like Kafka, but perfect, magnified. How much more is he able to transform the tragedies of our lives into a useful and purpose-filled story?

This is what he did in the life of Joseph. From infancy, Joseph was pressed by a number of thorns, some of them in the form of trauma, others in the form of chronic suffering. Born into a dysfunctional family (polygamy was fertile ground for jealousy and family tension), his mother died when he was about seven years old and his father spoiled him with such an ill-fated education that it aroused the envy and hatred of his brothers. When he was seventeen he faced the drama of being separated from his family at the height of adolescence, losing the only source of affection he had left, his father. Miraculously, he escaped death, first by being sold as a slave to the traders and then later in the incident with Potiphar's wife. All alone in Egypt, a foreign land, he suffered the consequences of slander, which sent him to prison for thirteen years.

The thorn of a childhood and youth filled with unjust suffering marked the first stage of his life. However, when years later he reviewed and evaluated all those events, he had an amazing awareness of God's presence and guidance in his life. Not only was God directing his steps, but he was also using every circumstance – good and bad – to fulfil his purpose in his life. His words to his brothers in Genesis 50:20 are a memorable summary of this trust: 'You intended to harm me, but God intended it for good.' And in Genesis 45:5–8 it is quite clear who led his life above and beyond his brothers' evil acts: ' . . . it was not you who sent me here, but God . . . ' It is difficult to read these passages without being deeply moved. Joseph had an unshakeable sense of God's providence: God allows, he directs, he liberates.

The interpretation that Stephen, inspired by the Holy Spirit, gave of these events in his message before being martyred is an excellent summary of everything seen up to this point. Stephen underscores three aspects of God's provision that constitute the essential strategy for fighting against the thorn. According to Acts 7:9–10, God gave Joseph:

- His constant presence: 'God was with him' (v. 9)
- Adequate ways out: God 'rescued him from all his troubles' (v. 10)
- Supernatural resources: 'God gave him wisdom' (v. 10).

Maturity: grace teaches

> To keep me from becoming conceited because of these surpassingly great
> revelations... (2 Corinthians 12:7).

The therapeutic effects of grace are progressive and interdependent, just like the links of a chain. The strength of grace enables a change of perspective and attitude. Eventually, the renewal of strength and the inner transformation lead to the third great therapeutic effect: that of teaching us important lessons. However, it is not the thorn that makes us grow, but our reactions as we face it.

In fact, this instructive value of suffering is recognized not only by believers. Renowned specialists in education and psychoanalysis have pointed to this for a long time. From Piaget to Françoise Dolto and other experts, we have become aware of how a child matures by resolving the little problems he faces along the way. Learning to face adversity is essential to the process of emotional maturity, so much so that the best way of keeping a person immature is to shield them from problems by providing them with a difficulty-free existence. Dostoevsky, in his autobiography *Memories from the Underground*, places a striking emphasis on the idea that suffering is an indispensable requisite for 'grasping the true sense of life'. Thorn-induced experiences are never futile: they always contain an instructive element that contributes to our emotional maturity. We would do well to remember this principle in a pleasure-driven society that sees no meaning or usefulness in suffering, considering it to be futile and thus opening the door to euthanasia or suicide.

In the same way that problems and difficulties contribute to our psychological maturity, so too they contribute to our spiritual growth. God uses trials as a means of transformation. This was the experience of Job, summarized in his memorable words: 'My ears had heard of you but now my eyes have seen you' (Job 42:5). The trials he went through allowed him to get to know God in a more personal way. In our case today, trials help us to become more like Christ. Let us not forget that the words *disciple* and *discipline* come from the same root, which means 'to instruct, to teach'. We must emphasize, nonetheless, that God's purpose in allowing suffering is not to punish but to teach. Thus, in the same way that rough stones taken from the quarry need to be cut and polished, so too we need to be sculpted to become more like Christ with each passing day. The Bible's teaching on this is overwhelming: numerous passages tell of the purifying and educational value of suffering, trials and temptations:

> No discipline seems pleasant at the time, but painful. Later on, however, it produces a harvest of righteousness and peace for those who have been trained by it (Hebrews 12:11).

> In this you greatly rejoice, though now for a little while you may have had to suffer grief in all kinds of trials. These have come so that your faith – of greater worth than gold, which perishes even though refined by fire – may be proved genuine and may result in praise, glory and honour when Jesus Christ is revealed (1 Peter 1:6–7).

The apostle Paul had experienced in his own life the transforming effect of trials. His writings and his own life remind us that the ability to face suffering without fleeing from it is a moral virtue that opens doors to our inner transformation. What did Paul have to learn from his thorn? One great lesson in particular: the danger of boasting and the need to remain humble.

Humility, the main lesson

The apostle had so clearly come to terms with the purpose of the thorn that he starts off the passage with these words: 'To keep me from becoming conceited because of these surpassingly great revelations' (2 Corinthians 12:7). The revelations he has spoken about in verses 1–6 are a double-edged sword: on the one hand they were an immense privilege, something very special that undoubtedly placed him above other believers; but therein also lay the danger: they were a potential source of pride and could arouse a feeling of spiritual superiority, in stark contrast to the attitude that the Lord desired. God could not let one of the pillars of the church, the apostle to the Gentiles, succumb to one of the most deeply-rooted sins in the human heart, pride. That is why God uses the great learning power of the thorn to show Paul his mistake and potential sin.

Sometimes we find ourselves in similarly dangerous situations. They will probably not involve special revelations through which we might feel very privileged by the Lord. However, whether it is in the professional, material or even spiritual arena, success inevitably leads to a great danger: boasting, when we forget that 'every good and perfect gift' comes from God (James 1:17). Boasting is a subtle sin that can sometimes appear in the guise of spirituality. That is where Paul's danger lay, in spiritual superiority. Temptation tends to make its appearance during times of success, when things are going very well for us.

Of course we cannot generalize from Paul's particular situation and claim that the purpose of *every* thorn is always to restrain our boasting. I have known countless individuals oppressed by a painful thorn who did not have even a hint of arrogance. However, it is true that the thorn helps us to be fully aware of our personal limitations, reminding us of the enormous fragility of our lives. In summary, not all thorns stem from an attitude of boasting, but all thorns help us to cultivate the humility that the Lord loves so much: 'This is the one I esteem: he who is humble and contrite in spirit' (Isaiah 66:2). In Christ, certainly when I am weak, then I am strong.

5 Angels along my path: the love that heals

Love is the principal, the paramount, the pre-eminent, the distinguishing characteristic of the people of God. Nothing can dislodge or replace it. Love is supreme.[1]

What role does love play in the struggle against the thorn? Up to this point we have considered some of the therapeutic effects of grace. Maybe you are wondering why I have not yet mentioned love. Love is the highest expression of grace. That is why it needs a chapter all of its own. *Grace is love in action and love originates in and feeds on grace.* The supreme example of this inseparable relationship between grace and love is found in the person of Jesus Christ: he is the paradigm of grace incarnated in love. Beautiful Bible verses remind us of this reality: 'For God so loved the world that he gave his one and only Son...' (John 3:16), or 'He who did not spare his own Son, but gave him up for us all – how will he not also, along with him, graciously give us all things?' (Romans 8:32).

Let us respond to two practical questions: who are the transmitters of this love and how does it show itself in its relationship to the thorn?

Who? The transmitters of grace

For a life in the dark, love is the surest guide.[2]

God uses key people, deeply meaningful in our lives, to help us fight against the thorn. They are specific people, with real names, who are like angels along our desert paths bringing us, above all, love. They are the transmitters of God's grace, because grace is not only something experienced, but also something shared. Grace is received, but it also needs to be transmitted. God never intended grace to be an individual experience, no matter how edifying it might be. We considered earlier how Jonathan was used by God to help David. Paul also had his 'angels' who helped him in his most difficult moments. It is exciting to see how the apostle refers to Epaphroditus as 'my brother, fellow-worker and fellow-soldier, who is also your messenger, whom you sent to take care of my needs' (Philippians 2:25) and who 'almost died for the work of Christ, risking his life to make up for the help you could not give me' (v. 30).

In our situation, where are we going to find these servant transmitters of God's grace and love? Of course, God can use the person we least expect. Life is full of examples of anonymous men and women whose generosity, compassion and altruism are reminders of the divine image that every human being retains as an indelible imprint on their hearts. Nonetheless, there are certain spheres in which we are more likely to find these 'angel' transmitters of grace and love. We will consider two of them: on the one hand, family and friends, and, on the other hand, the church – what we call the 'supernatural help' because it contains ingredients that go beyond mere natural support.

Family and friends: the natural help

Our main support should obviously come from those who are closest to us – family and friends. Their love, commitment and empathy are irreplaceable. In fact, the thorn very often affects the entire family, parents, siblings and children, who suffer as much as the person directly affected, especially when the thorn touches a child, for example with a disability or a chronic illness. Although the parents and siblings do not literally suffer from the problem, in practice they do experience it as if it were their own. This is the high cost that comes with an identification that is as natural as it is necessary. Family life is like a delicate system of communicating vessels in which everything affects everyone. In fact, the emotional wear and tear that these situations create for caregivers – particularly the closest family members – makes it highly advisable that they also receive help. The classic question 'Who cares for the carer?' takes on a particular relevance here. Much of this book's content is applicable as much to close relatives as it is to the person living with the thorn. Every day the family needs to experience the refreshing and renewing breeze of grace that in turn enables each member to continue giving that same grace to their suffering relative.

The lack of such support from closest family members is a major handicap in the acceptance process. Besides, it can cause fractures in communication with family members or among friends. This happened, for example, with Job: what his broken heart needed most was the support of his wife and friends, but he was soon to discover that those who should have been a balm for his wounds became in fact like vinegar. Instead of bringing hope, they brought irritation and disconsolation. Truly there is nothing better than a period of pain to test the levels of love and friendship. 'A friend loves at all times, and a brother is born for adversity', we are reminded in the wisdom of Proverbs (Proverbs 17:17).

Suffering often provides good opportunities for strengthening relationships, but it is also a time of danger. When the storm rages, the bond of love can be reinforced, but dangerous leaks can also appear, letting the water in. Numerous studies have shown that the unexpected appearance of a thorn can detonate a crisis in a marriage. We must keep up our guard and think not only about the needs of the affected person but also of those of their spouse, children, and so on. I remember a woman who, weeping, told me, 'When our son was born – with cerebral palsy – somehow I lost my husband. It was like a wall that rose up between us. It wasn't that he shied away from caring for the boy – he did take care of him and did everything that would be normal in the situation. But he didn't have anything to do with me: he abandoned me emotionally. When I needed him the most, he inexplicably distanced himself. My loneliness became unbearable.'

This woman's sad experience can help us outline some of the basic needs of the person dealing with a thorn,[3] without forgetting that their family members have needs too.

- Companionship: emotional support
- Empathy: feeling understood
- Practical support: help in facing the new challenges that appear with the thorn. This is especially true in the adaptation phase, when one must learn to live differently
- Hope: the sense that life will regain its meaning and there is a future.

In fact, these four needs converge in a single one that can be defined in negative terms: *not feeling alone*. Loneliness is always hard to accept because people are not born for isolation but for relationship. However, loneliness is particularly painful at the time of the thorn. We should do our absolute best to make sure that the person suffering from the thorn – and his or her closest caregivers – should not feel like the Psalmist, who wrote, 'My heart is blighted and withered like grass . . . I am like a desert owl, like an owl among the ruins. I lie awake; I have become like a bird alone on a housetop' (Psalm 102:4, 6–7). This leads us to consider another great resource of grace, the church.

Church, the supernatural support

For believers there is also another family, a family of families, which is a unique setting for experiencing love and grace: the church. How can the local church help the person suffering from a thorn, and also help their family? Above all, by offering them grace. *Grace is the most distinctive contribution the church can make* to those stricken by a thorn. Grace strengthens, encourages, comforts. In his excellent book *What's So Amazing About Grace?*, Philip Yancey quotes Gordon MacDonald: 'The world can do almost anything as well as or better than the church . . . There is only one thing the world cannot do. It cannot offer grace.'[4]

Biblical teaching is emphatic about the idea that we are a body and belong to one another: 'Now you are the body of Christ, and each one of you is a part of it . . . its parts should have equal concern for each other . . . If one part suffers, every part suffers with it; if one part is honoured, every part rejoices with it' (1 Corinthians 12:25–27).

The Christian life is not a matter of 'God and me alone'. A solitary Christian is incompatible with New Testament teaching. Faith does of course have an intimate and personal dimension that must be respected, but it goes far beyond the private realm, with inevitable community and social implications. John Wesley often reminded his listeners of a friend's words: 'The Bible knows nothing of solitary religion.'[5] Whether we like it or not, when we experience the new birth – conversion – we come to form part of a family in which, just as in any other family, we do not have the right to choose our siblings. (I have never yet met anyone who has had the opportunity to choose his or her blood siblings!)

Thus being a support community is in the very nature of the church. Its natural solidarity – 'for we are all members of one body' (Ephesians 4:25) – is strengthened by the supernatural love of grace: 'because God has poured out his love into our hearts by the Holy Spirit, whom he has given us' (Romans 5:5). The love of Christ is the motivation that 'compels us' (2 Corinthians 5:14). Indeed, it impels us to love those suffering from a thorn and their families. The church becomes a support community. This was such a natural characteristic of the church in the early centuries that the first hospitals were founded by Christians. As a matter of fact the concept of *hospital* is inseparably joined to Christianity. Concern for the sick was something so natural and accepted among Christians in the Middle Ages that a hospital was always built next to every monastery, as can be seen even today. Of course these hospitals were very different from hospitals today; they were used primarily for sufferers from leprosy, the blind, the infirm and the marginalized – in other words, men and women fighting against gruelling thorns.

Today, even non-believing professionals have admitted the relevant role that Christian communities can play in helping suffering people. This is one of the merits that the church can offer our society today. In a world where the family is in crisis and no longer constitutes a safe refuge, the local church is an alternative family. A church where members bear one another's burdens becomes a home, a family of families through which God 'provides homes for those who are deserted' (Psalm 68:6, HCSB).

The church can be a healing community, a therapeutic instrument for a hurting world. Many people today who are discouraged owing to distress, depression or loneliness, hurt by broken relationships or dire family situations, wander through life as 'injured' and 'weak' (Ezekiel 34:16). It is these people who, exhausted by thorns, will make their way to a church in search of someone who will share their burdens. We must be on the lookout for them, willing to carry their 'knapsack' for a while, i.e. listen to them, understand them and, above all, love them with the love of Christ who showed a deep interest in all who were 'in need of a doctor'. Grace, expressed in love, should be the distinctive mark of a church that is alive.

How? Healing through love

We have considered the *who*, the transmitters of grace and love. Now we must focus on the *how*. How do we go about giving the support, the empathy, the practical help and the hope that are so vital? We could make a list of useful and commonsense suggestions. But this kind of information can easily be found in any counselling or self-help book. Because my desire throughout this book is to let the Word of God speak as much as possible, I prefer to focus on two exhortations from the apostolic teaching which are a mine of rich material on the practice of Christian love:

> Carry each other's burdens, and in this way you will fulfil the law of Christ (Galatians 6:2).

> Stir up one another to love (Hebrews 10: 24, ESV).

'Carry each other's burdens'

In this verse we find not only valuable psychological wisdom but also one of the most healing effects of grace. Grace is the supernatural strength that enables us to carry each other's burdens, and, even though Paul's exhortation is directed at the church, it also applies to individuals, including the family and close friends of the suffering person.

Let us notice, first of all, that this verse is a command, not an option. The verb 'carry' is an imperative. If we belong to one another, the natural consequence is to 'carry each other's burdens'. Caring for our brothers and sisters is not only a privilege to enjoy, but a duty to accomplish. Young's Literal Translation (1898) accurately conveys the emphasis: 'of one another the burdens bear ye.' Paul places 'of one another' in the genitive at the beginning of the sentence to indicate its emphasis.

So how do we practise this exhortation? The word 'carry' or 'bear' is the same as in John 19:17, when Jesus carried his own cross and started making his way to Golgotha. The idea conveyed in the original is that of carrying 'something that weighs heavily'. The same word for 'burden', *baros*, is used in Matthew 20:12, referring to the work and tiring nature of the day: 'And you have made them equal to us who have borne the burden of the work and the heat of the day.' So it can mean both a physical and a symbolic or moral weight – something that is burdensome and oppressive, such as a worry, a problem, a hardship or an illness.

I would like to illustrate this idea: all of us are travelling through life carrying knapsacks of different weights. The idea of 'carrying one another's burdens' refers to taking your neighbour's knapsack and carrying it for a while. That is exactly what Simon did when the Roman soldiers made him carry Jesus' cross because Jesus was more than likely completely exhausted: 'They seized Simon from Cyrene, who was on his way in from the country, and put the cross on him and made him carry it behind Jesus' (Luke 23:26). What a privilege for Simon to share Jesus' burden! Likewise, the word used in Isaiah 53:4 – 'Surely he took up our infirmities and carried our sorrows' – is the same one as in Galatians 6:2 – '*carry* each other's burdens'. In the very act of carrying – and dying on – that cross, Jesus was bearing all our sins.

Obviously there is one sense in which we cannot carry the burdens of our neighbour as Jesus did: the substitutionary, vicarious element of the Lord's death that cannot be repeated. But, in a broader sense, we can and we ought to imitate Christ. The very life of Jesus impels us to do the same. In fact, the word 'law', which appears in the second part of the verse 'in this way you will fulfil the law of Christ', does not mean *precept* so much as *model*. It refers to the spirit, character and demeanour of Christ, who, 'anointed ... with the Holy Spirit and power ... went around doing good and healing all ...' (Acts 10:38). Every believer should desire to have this pastoral heart that causes us to approach a brother or sister and ask, 'What's the matter? Can I do something for you? Can I carry your knapsack for a while?'

'Stirring up one another to love'

This second exhortation is placed in a context that accurately describes more practical ways of sharing the other person's burden: 'And let us consider how to stir up one another to love and good works, not neglecting to meet together, as is the habit of some, but encouraging one another' (Hebrews 10:24–25). Notice the emphasis again on the Christian life as an experience to be lived as a body: 'not neglecting to meet together'. Individual efforts are important, but they are not enough if love and good works are to be promoted.

Let us focus on the first sentence ' ... how to stir up one another to love'. The word for 'stirring up', *paroxysmos*, is a significant term meaning 'to incite'. As Donald Guthrie puts it, 'it seems to suggest that loving one another will not just happen. It needs to be worked out, even provoked'.[6]

If we compare love to a fire, both starting and maintaining a fire require effort and a watchful attitude. The idea is to be proactive in showing concern for and promoting the good of my neighbour. It simply means taking the other person into account, not ignoring him or her. Sometimes a sincere and heartfelt 'How are you?' suffices to show our love. At other times, words may be unnecessary and the same attitude of love is communicated through a penetrating and comforting gaze that speaks for itself, silently saying, 'Can I be of any help to you? I'm by your side if you need me.' A handwritten note or postcard at special moments, a phone call or a visit to their home are other practical ways of *considering one another* that communicate valuable support to the person suffering with a thorn.

Also, we should not forget that one of the most effective ways of carrying the burdens is by *listening* to the other person. Listening carefully, not only with our ears but with our eyes, conveys a powerful message of love. Remember the story of Job's 'comforters': talking too much was the main source of the mistakes they made. This is why God rebuked them at the end: 'I am angry with you and your two friends, because you have not spoken ... what is right ... ' (Job 42:7). If they had remained silent, as they did for the first few days (see 2:13), and just listened to Job's laments, their comfort to the tormented Job would have been much more effective. In suffering, love is expressed much better by the warmth of a caring hand than by the eloquence of a long discourse.

Finally, this exhortation clearly refers to the *reciprocal* dimension of love. It is striking to see how in the New Testament there are more than fifty commandments that include the phrase 'one another': love one another, comfort one another, encourage one another, serve one another, bear with one another, forgive one another ... as reciprocal commandments. There is no place for a passive attitude within the church. It is always a matter of giving and receiving. All these attitudes – works of love – are a practical expression of the grace of Christ. People suffering with a thorn need to experience this grace, made visible in their spiritual family. Love is like a fire with limitless energy. Undoubtedly it is the key ingredient in grace to transform people, relationships and situations. Hence its sterling value for helping the person dealing with a thorn.

Prayers that support: the therapeutic value of my brothers' and sisters' prayers

> . . . we were so utterly burdened beyond our strength . . . you also joined in helping us through your prayers (2 Corinthians 1:8, 11, ESV/NASB).

One of the most powerful ways we can show our support is through prayer. To pray *for* and *with* the person or family that suffers from a thorn has a soothing effect and constitutes an unfailing source of comfort. When someone prays for me, I feel accompanied, understood and supported. This is especially true in the initial stages of the thorn, when it seems that the world is crashing in on us. But also later on, when we have genuinely come to accept the problem, intercession by our Christian family continues to be important for experiencing renewed forces of grace. Paul referred to this idea in an emotive passage:

> We know that as you share in our sufferings, you will also share in our comfort. For we were so utterly burdened beyond our strength that we despaired of life itself. Indeed, we felt that we had received the sentence of death (2 Corinthians 1:7–9, ESV).

And the apostle continues, sharing what their prayers had meant to him in such dire straits: 'He has delivered us from such a deadly peril, and he will deliver us. On him we have set our hope that he will continue to deliver us, as you help us by your prayers' (vv. 10–11). The force of this passage is surprising, for Paul is in effect saying, 'When you pray for me in my tribulation, you are fighting alongside me, helping me.'

And it is not merely of psychological benefit that 'someone has remembered me'. Prayer does not operate as a placebo or a self-suggestion technique but by its enormous spiritual power. Prayer can change circumstances, but it also changes people, a phenomenon that medicine has studied in depth over recent years, with surprising results.

Several independent research projects have shown how those patients who prayed or knew that others were praying for them (for example, after having an operation or going through cancer treatment) had a faster and better recovery rate than other patients who did not have prayer backing. Exactly the same thing occurs when suffering from a thorn.

The source of grace: 'I can do all things in Christ who strengthens me'

> Remain in me, and I will remain in you ... apart from me you can do nothing (John 15:4–5).

So far we have seen some of the transmitters of grace: the family, the church, friends: instruments in God's hands to dispense grace. In the words of the apostle Peter, they are 'good stewards of God's varied grace' (1 Peter 4:10, ESV). The spring from which this divine gift flows is Christ himself, which is why grace is inseparable from a **personal relationship with Christ**. We receive this grace when we are in intimate communion with Christ, just as a plant receives its vital life sap from the main trunk. There are no shortcuts or substitutes. Herein lies the essence of acceptance: *it is a supernatural spiritual experience*. If I want to experience God's grace, I have to cultivate my relationship with Christ.

Let us now return to 2 Corinthians 12, the text dealing with the thorn. Between verses 8 and 10, where Paul's transformation takes place, there is a phrase worth noting. Seemingly insignificant, it contains nothing less than the secret *par excellence* of this profound change: '... *but he [the Lord] said to me*' (v. 9). It is not by his own efforts or through a personal process of psychological maturity that Paul comes to have an attitude of joyful acceptance, but in response to the encounter he has had with his Lord in prayer. Paul has *known* God's answer in the Hebrew sense, that is, he has experientially known what God has told him. This is not mere informational knowledge. It reminds us again of the Old Testament prophet Habakkuk, a man who also fought intensely with God in prayer. After hearing God's answer, and as an introduction to a memorable prayer, Habakkuk affirms: 'O LORD, I have heard your speech and was afraid' (Habakkuk 3:2, NKJV). From the content of this prayer we see how God's answer had changed the prophet's attitudes, thoughts and feelings. The apostle's experience with regard to the thorn is the same.

The explanation of this spiritual reality is seen in Philippians 4:11–13, the text that was the basis for our discussion of contentment: 'I have learned to be content ... I can do all things **through Christ** who strengthens me...'. Verses 11 and 13 are inseparable. There is no true contentment without Christ. This is the key to accepting the thorn and also to the entire Christian life. Famous people can encourage me by their example, inspiring me. The power of Christ goes much further than being an *inspiration*; he performs a *transformation* which energizes me on the inside, enabling me to face any situation. Christ is able to strengthen me because he is truly alive today and his power is delivered to me as the vine gives sap to the branches.

In the original, the preposition Paul uses is *in*: 'I can do all things IN Christ'. It does not say 'with' or 'by' Christ. It is an existential position. It is not a sporadic experience, intense as this might be, but a permanent relationship. It is not an occasional encounter, like that of a patient with a psychologist or counsellor that enables the patient to leave after the therapy session 'feeling encouraged and uplifted'. Contentment is possible only when we are in Christ because the sap will flow through the branch only if it is connected to the vine.

How does Christ strengthen me?
In the light of biblical teaching, Christ meets the three main needs of the person suffering from a thorn, which we described earlier.

- **Christ is beside me: his companionship**. The last words spoken by Jesus before returning to heaven were: 'Surely I am with you always, to the very end of the age' (Matthew 28:20). The author of the epistle to the Hebrews likewise quotes God's promise to Joshua, applying it to every believer: 'Never will I leave you; never will I forsake you' (Hebrews 13:5), the consequence of which is very encouraging: 'So we say with confidence, "The Lord is my helper; I will not be afraid. What can man do to me?"' (v. 6). His companionship, his presence, is the source of encouragement and strengthening.

    This was the experience of Henrietta, a woman who had spent fifteen years in a wheelchair after an accident had left her quadriplegic. She could not move her arms or legs at all. Her grandchildren, impressed by her immobility, wondered what she thought about all day long because she was always calm and peaceful. She shared her secret in a nutshell: 'If I didn't have my Lord Jesus at my side, I'd ask that my days be shortened!'

The comfort of Christ's presence is expressed in the matchless lyrics of a hymn that, some time ago, was chosen in a survey as one of the ten most-loved hymns by Christians in the United States:

> Abide with me, fast falls the eventide.
> The darkness deepens; Lord, with me abide.
> When other helpers fail and comforts flee,
> Help of the helpless, O abide with me.
>
> I need Thy presence every passing hour;
> What but Thy grace can foil the tempter's power?
> Who like Thyself my guide and stay can be?
> Through cloud and sunshine O abide with me.

- **Christ suffers with me: his empathy**. Another great need of the person suffering from a thorn is to *feel understood*. And who can better understand than the person who has previously gone through a similar experience? God's participation in and identification with human suffering is unfathomable but at the same time it is what offers the greatest comfort to the suffering person. In the moving description of the sufferings of Christ in Isaiah 53 lies the ultimate answer to all suffering: 'he was despised . . . he was pierced . . . he was crushed . . . he was oppressed and afflicted, yet he did not open his mouth; he was led like a lamb to the slaughter.' So much suffering had a purpose: 'by his wounds we are healed . . . after the suffering of his soul, he will see the light of life and be satisfied . . . for he bore the sin of many, and made intercession for the transgressors.'

For all these reasons, because he was an *expert*[7] in suffering, 'we do not have a high priest who is unable to sympathise with our weaknesses, but we have one who has been tempted in every way, just as we are – yet was without sin' (Hebrews 4:15). Here also the author concludes in a passionate exhortation: 'Let us then approach the throne of grace with confidence, so that we may receive mercy and find grace to help us in our time of need' (v. 16).

I quote this again deliberately because it describes amazingly the close association between our relationship with Christ – 'let us then approach' – and the grace dispensed by the 'time of need', that is to say, the necessary help, which I need at that very moment. Christ gives me not only his companionship but also his full understanding in view of my trial. He understands me because he has already experienced the pain and anguish of the thorn.

- **Christ intercedes for me: his prayers.** Intercession for each one of us is another activity that Christ is engaged in right now, while seated at the right hand of the Father. We read in Romans 8:34, 'Who is he that condemns? Christ Jesus, who died – more than that, who was raised to life – is at the right hand of God and is also interceding for us.' And in Hebrews 7:25 the Lord is presented as one who 'always lives to intercede for [us]'. As we saw earlier, the prayers of our church family do us a lot of good because they communicate *support* to us, which is another great need of the afflicted person. Prayer also covers the other two needs, companionship and empathy. It makes us feel at the same time supported and understood as we live with our thorn. If all this is true with regard to the prayers of our Christian siblings, how much more must Jesus' intercession on our behalf comfort us? For me this was one of the most revolutionary discoveries in my struggle with a thorn: to know and feel that every day Christ is interceding for me personally. This is the best antidote to discouragement in the daily struggle with my thorn.

Growing in grace

If you know there is a medicine that heals, you will do everything possible to take it. So, as our final consideration, how do we receive this transforming grace?

Grace is not something that is obtained once and for all. It is not like a fixed capital that does not vary. This is why the Bible uses one verb to describe grace as something dynamic and constantly renewed: 'to grow'. Of the Lord Jesus it is said, for example, that he grew 'in grace with God and men' (Luke 2:52, literal translation by the author from the original Greek). Peter exhorts us to 'grow in the grace and knowledge of our Lord and Saviour Jesus Christ' (2 Peter 3:18). Similarly, Paul exhorts

Timothy, 'You then, my son, be strong in the grace that is in Christ Jesus' (2 Timothy 2:1).

Even though we may have reached an excellent level of acceptance, comparable to that of the apostle Paul who rejoiced in his weakness, our need of grace does not disappear but rather is constant. This is logical. We are talking about situations of prolonged suffering in which the thorn is not removed. Many things have changed, though God's answer has not been to remove the thorn but to give us the resources necessary to cope with it. As a result, just as a person with a chronic illness needs permanent treatment, we have to continue to take the divine medicine that invigorates us: 'my grace is sufficient for you.' Thus, the spiritual experience of grace is not like an antibiotic that one takes for several days and that's it. No. Grace is rather like the eye drops that the patient needs to apply daily to his sore eyes. Discipline, perseverance and effort are required. We depend on grace to be well. It is indeed a marvellous dependence!

On the other hand, the idea of growth is a reminder that the **forms** of experiencing grace can be diverse. There will be special moments of intense fellowship with the Lord, moments that will leave an unforgettable memory. Such was Jacob's experience at Peniel. Every believer has some of these stellar moments that serve as milestones in his or her relationship with God. However, generally speaking, growth develops in a continual and gradual way, similar to the way a child develops physically and psychologically. Grace is like the sediment that a river deposits on its bed almost imperceptibly. With time, however, the sediment becomes quite noticeable. This is what mostly happens in our spiritual growth.

There is one final issue. The growth process in grace, and in the acceptance of the thorn, is not immune from oscillation or from apparent setbacks. It is never a straight, upward line, free from doubts and relapses into rebellion and protest. There are moments of defeat in which a person feels they have lost everything they have gained. These are moments when, for some reason, it seems that we are fighting in vain. We row with all our strength but the wind blows strongly against us and the waves prevent us from advancing. We ask ourselves whether indeed we have advanced at all.

A diagram can help us understand this concept better. Figure 1 shows what we might call 'never-failing' growth, without relapse, always in a straight, upward line. This kind of growth is unreal and reflects a non-biblical triumphalism. The struggle against the thorn does not operate

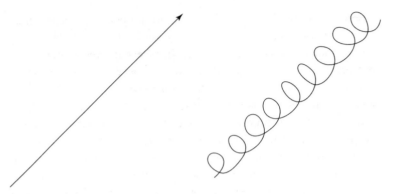

Figure 1. 'Never-failing' growth   Figure 2. 'Spiral' growth

this way. On the other hand, Figure 2 shows growth in a 'spiral' fashion. There are ups and downs, but what is significant is that the relapses never return to the original starting point; there is clearly a growth process.

Finding grace in your own life

If the source of grace is in Christ, how can we cultivate the personal relationship considered above? What enables us to stay *in him*? A detailed treatment of this is beyond the scope of this book,[8] so I will simply outline the answer:

Reading and meditating on the Word of God

The study of God's Word enables us not only to know the truth but also to meet the True One, the One who said, 'I am the way, the truth and the life.' Seek to imitate the Christians of Berea, who 'received the message with great eagerness and examined the Scriptures every day' (Acts 17:11) and you will have an encounter with the living Christ. The Scriptures are filled with Christ: 'And beginning with Moses and all the Prophets, he explained to them what was said in all the Scriptures concerning himself' (Luke 24:27).

- Allow the Word to speak to you personally
- Allow the Word to penetrate in your heart, that it may 'dwell in you richly'
- Allow the Word to change and fashion you.

For the word of God is living and active. Sharper than any double-edged sword, it penetrates even to dividing soul and spirit, joints and marrow; it judges the thoughts and attitudes of the heart (Hebrews 4:12).

Prayer

We have considered the value of the prayers of our brothers and sisters. What about our own prayers? Prayer is a most powerful instrument because it allows us to converse with God as our Father, naturally and intimately, knowing that he is the 'Abba' – Daddy – of whom Paul speaks to us (Romans 8:15). It is in prayer, more than anywhere else, that God ceases to be a distant 'it' and becomes the nearby and knowable 'Thou' of whom the German-Jewish philosopher Martin Buber wrote.[9] 'In prayer one does not limit oneself to talking *to* God; one must speak *with* God, *coram Deo*, face to face with him.'[10]

If meditating on the Word implies listening to God, allowing him to speak to you, prayer is where you speak to God. But, even without realizing it, the Lord also uses this tool to mould us, to make us grow. Prayer has the power to change circumstances, but it also changes us. As Richard Foster has said, 'Prayer is change. Prayer is the main avenue that God uses to transform us.'[11] We have all experienced at one time or another how anxiety is replaced by the peace 'that passes all understanding'; hatred and resentment by an attitude of forgiveness and even love; fear by trust; doubt by certainty, when we present ourselves before God with a sincere heart 'in everything, by prayer and petition, with thanksgiving' (Philippians 4:6). Because 'prayer is the vital factor of faith, the believer prays. The person who prays, believes'.[12]

These are the precious stones contained in the manifold grace of God. It is in personal application that the ultimate secret of the acceptance of the thorn is found. What amazing power is offered to us by the one who was able to bring the dead back to life!

6 Recovering the joy of living: new values for a different life

Personally, I believe there is no life so degraded, spoiled or impoverished that it does not deserve respect, or that is not worth defending.[1]

Can you be happy again after the trials of life have buffeted you? Is the 'thorn in the flesh' like a life sentence that prevents you from ever seeing the sun shining again? We have already answered this question in part. In chapters 3 and 4 we looked at contentment and joy, which are deeper than a mere feeling, at acceptance and at struggling serenely, but does grace also bring happiness? Can the person hurt by a thorn recover the joy of living?

The answer is an unequivocal 'yes'. Paraphrasing a well-known saying, 'There's life after the thorn!' Reading through the biographies of people who have been afflicted with severe trials, it has been tremendously encouraging to me to discover how these men and women were able to rise from the ashes of their own existence and live new lives full of meaning, not *in spite of* very great limitations, but actually *because of* them. Their thorns were what drove them in their new lives.

We should mention here the extraordinary case of the American Helen Keller (1880–1968), who was blind, deaf and mute from the age of two as the result of disease. Her education and training are considered the most amazing accomplishment ever achieved by a handicapped person.

Helen not only learned to read, write and talk, but became exceptionally proficient in her studies. I want to quote two of her sayings, which are a reminder of this incredible capacity to recover the joy of living in spite of severe limitations: 'In every limitation we overcome, and in the higher ideals we thus attain, the whole kingdom of love and wisdom is present.'[2] 'The joy of surmounting obstacles that once seemed irremovable ... what other joy is there like it?'[3]

Yes, some of the best evidence that someone has reached an adequate level of acceptance is the recovery of a certain *joie de vivre*. And grace is 'sufficient for us' in this respect too because it gives us the necessary resources to live a full life. This is why it seems appropriate to devote this final chapter to the subject of the meaning of life, and to happiness. First, we will see what the Bible considers to be a happy life, and then look at the ingredients that go to make it up.

What is happiness? Blessed or fortunate?

> The secret of happiness is not always doing what one wants, but always wanting what one does (Leo Tolstoy).

> Blessed is the man ...
> [whose] delight is in the law of the LORD.
> (Ps 1:1–2)

We often hear people say 'the most important thing in life is to be happy'. But is happiness a priority for the believer? Happiness has become an untouchable idol before which millions kneel, an idol that justifies any behaviour or decision, from divorce – 'I've got the right to be happy' – to the most excessive consumerism. Advertising experts understand this well and make the most of this thirst for happiness by promoting their products with the guarantee that they will take people to the 'promised land' of happiness.

What do we understand by 'happiness'? It is beyond the bounds of this book to offer a detailed analysis, but we do need some basic ideas to apply to the issue of the thorn. Let's note in the first instance, its popular meaning. It is striking that in some languages the word 'happiness' includes a root meaning *luck* or *chance*. For instance, the English prefix *hap-* denotes 'being lucky'. The world considers a happy person to be one who has had good luck in their life. But 'luck' with what?

The contemporary view of happiness is strongly influenced by hedonism and materialism. Most people associate being happy with the possession of lots of material goods, the lack of illness, and success in relationships, especially those involving love. An ancient Spanish saying puts it like this: 'There are three things in life: health, wealth and love.' However, if we allow ourselves to go down this line, the person with a thorn in the flesh is condemned to being unhappy all their life because thorns have a profound effect on one of these areas, and maybe even on all three at the same time.

If being happy is not suffering or having problems, having as good a time as possible and achieving every target you set yourself in the area of personal ambition, then most of us will never be happy. Yet this is the concept constantly and brazenly offered by everyone from the media to politicians, including psychiatrists and doctors. Perhaps this is one of the reasons why the incidence of suicide in the West has increased so alarmingly in recent years that in 2003 UK government statistics ranked it as the second most frequent cause of death in men and women aged between fifteen and thirty-four.

Such a view is not merely Utopian, but is based on flimsy values, like a house built on sand. The Austrian philosopher Ernst Fischer shrewdly describes the emptiness of human happiness when he says, 'Our happiness appears in the silence of the reflection of nothing.' Human happiness is full of nothing. How such nihilism differs from the fullness that springs from the One who said: 'I have come that you may have life, and life to the full' (John 10:10). The **biblical concept** of happiness is very different from the popular one outlined above. What does it consist of? The terms used in the original languages are very revealing. In the Old Testament, the Hebrew word *shalah* or *shalav*, translated 'happiness' (cf. Jeremiah 12:1), means 'to be safe', 'to be at rest'. The singularity of the biblical concept is found in its close relationship with the Hebrew word for 'peace', *shalom*, the two terms having a common root, *shal*. Etymology reminds us of the closeness of two facts: happiness is inseparable from peace, a peace that is not merely the absence of war, problems or suffering, but a state of well-being reflected in inner contentment and harmony in one's personal relationships, a state of well-being akin to the harmony of an orchestra when all its component parts play in tune. True happiness is a state of inner peace that is much more than just a feeling.

What's more, in a biblical sense, happiness and peace are defined in positive terms and give an integral vision of the person, seeing human beings as a unity. They remind us, therefore, that the concept of health is not merely the *absence* of illness. It is interesting to note that the World Health Organization was inspired by this Hebrew idea when it formulated its definition of health: 'Health is the state of physical, mental and social well-being, and not just the absence of illness.'

In the New Testament the term used is *makarios*, which is translated as 'happy' or 'blessed'. The latter translation is the one that appears in the Sermon on the Mount when Jesus gives the Beatitudes. This is a very special word. It was used to describe the ancient Greek gods. Curiously, it was also the adjective used to name the island we know as Cyprus, alluding to its agreeable climate and rich natural resources, as well as its natural beauty. It contained *within its borders* all necessary resources, so that one did not need to leave the island to be happy. Referring to this idea of the 'happy island', W. Barclay writes: '*Makarios* then describes that joy which has its secret within itself, that joy which is serene and untouchable, that joy which is completely independent of all the chances and all the changes of life.'[4]

It is important to note once again that, in both Old and New Testaments, happiness is presented as something that comes from God. It is not a human resource, but a supernatural one. The source of happiness, just as in the case of peace, a fruit of the Spirit, is found in a personal relationship with God. 'Blessed (happy) is the man ... (whose) delight is in the law of the LORD, and on his law he meditates day and night' (Psalm 1:1–2). The Psalm reminds us that this happiness is not dissipated by the storms of life because it is 'like a tree planted by streams of water' (v. 3). Happiness, according to God, is strong and deep-rooted.

A much-afflicted Paul describes this idea with great energy shortly before the passage about the thorn in the flesh:

> ... sorrowful, yet always rejoicing; poor, yet making many rich; having nothing, yet possessing everything ... I am greatly encouraged; in all our troubles my joy knows no bounds (2 Corinthians 6:10; 7:4).

Happiness, experienced through peace and harmony even in the midst of trouble, is one of the greatest proofs that the thorn in the flesh has been accepted.

A man who was almost blind and had had a foot amputated owing to diabetes summed it up well with these words: 'The thorn has crushed many of my hopes, but has not been able to crush my joy in living.'

The ingredients of happiness: a new set of values

Set your minds on things above, not on earthly things (Colossians 3:2).

Grace changes many things in the fight against the thorn in the flesh. We have seen how it changes our viewpoint, generating new attitudes, and how it gives strength and helps us grow in maturity. To everything we described in chapters four and five we must add one more effect: **it gives us a new set of values**. Our priorities, goals and motivation will never be the same again. In part, this is down to the thorn itself: one cannot view life in the same way after the impact of the thorn, but, above all, it is the result of grace, of that transforming process that allows us to discover opportunities where previously we had seen only problems.

Grace changes our view not only of the thorn, but of the whole of life. When Paul affirms 'therefore I will boast the more gladly', he has learnt not only acceptance, but a completely different set of values for his life. In the case of someone pricked by the thorn, this set of values will be notable for two priorities:

- the priority of being
- the priorities of a pilgrim.

Being before doing: the priority of being in a society of doing

Sow a thought, reap an action; sow an action, reap a habit; sow a habit, reap a character; sow a character, reap a destiny (traditional saying).

One of the greatest frustrations caused by the thorn is 'not being able to do what you did before'. It imposes limitations, suddenly or gradually, on your normal activities, and this often leads to unhappiness and depression. *'What I found hardest was giving up what I used to be able* to do without anybody's help; work all day like everybody else, drive, shave, in a word, all those little things which make you feel alive. It was a tough process; finally I discovered that life was much more than doing; I had to learn to be.'

'I had to learn to be.' A difficult task in a society that values people more for what they *do* – their *productivity* – than for who they *are* – their *character.* These days life is lived under the slogan 'You're worth what you do'. In all areas of life, from work to church, there is frenetic activism. Efficiency and performance are stressed, as are concrete results. It seems that the only way to fill one's life is by *doing.* Such excessive activity involves a strange paradox: it has become a sign of identity – *a person who does nothing is a nobody* – and at the same time it is a subtle means of escape from oneself. Continual activity may easily become an escape route. It is almost like a drug, as the abstinence syndrome it produces goes to show: lots of people feel uncomfortable when they have nothing to do, as if something is missing from their lives. They do not know how to *be* without *doing.* We have been educated for action, but not for reflection. This situation makes the acceptance of, and adaptation to, thorns all the more difficult, because they force us to reduce our activity.

So how can we help someone whose thorn has forced them into a lifestyle far removed from that of most people? The key is to discover the value of *being* in a society of doing. We have already seen that our goal as human beings is to become more and more like Christ, and that a trial is an opportunity for strengthening character because it produces emotional and spiritual maturity. We are now going to go into this more deeply.

'His life was his best book'

This comment, which someone made about the Jewish Christian philosopher Emmanuel Levinas when he died, had a considerable impact on me. I thought about my own life. Can there be a better summary or tribute for a believer? It made me think about a biblical principle that has been a source of encouragement to me since I learnt it in my teenage years: the *most important thing in this life is not what we do, but who we are.* Each one of us is writing a book with our life. The most important chapters are not the achievements, qualifications or successes that are usually gained by doing. The essential part is *the person,* his or her character, reactions, relationships and development. 'For character is more than a collection of occasional behaviours or a set of good intentions; it is, rather, who we are through and through.'[5]

The thorn in the flesh may deprive me of many things, but it cannot prevent me from *being* a good husband, or *being* a good father, or *being* a good friend, or *being* a loving son or – and this is the most important of all – from *being* each day more like Christ. No one can take this from me because it does not depend on any outside circumstance, but upon my attitudes. We could paraphrase the beautiful love song of 1 Corinthians 13 and state that '*being never fails*'. Even though I achieve little in this life, I can continue to be a 'living letter' in which others read inspiring messages.

We transmit messages through our attitudes and reactions, and even through our silences. They might be positive messages, ones of encouragement, examples to follow, or they might be negative. A recent example in Spain was given by Enrique Medina, a young victim of a terrorist attack. The leader of the Young Socialists in the Basque Country, he lost a leg and suffered other serious injuries when a bomb exploded next to his car. Aged twenty, Enrique saw many of his dreams shattered, not least a brilliant career in volleyball, one of the loves of his life. His mother died ten months later from a heart attack clearly related to the sufferings endured by her family.

'After the bombing, night fell on my home and a shadow of sadness and grief wrapped itself around my family,' he said. At the trial, the press focused on the attitude of the young man with comments such as 'Enrique has taught us the most important lesson of his life, one of maturity and serenity'. All the journalists highlighted his attitude, his reactions and his character. The impact of his testimony was felt right across the nation.

'Do not consider his appearance . . . the LORD does not look at the things man looks at' (1 Samuel 16:7)

If this is what happens to us, how much more is it the case with God? For him, the most important thing is what we are like rather than what we do, because God tests 'the heart and mind' (Jeremiah 11:20). The whole of Scripture teaches the idea that attitudes come before actions. Let's look at a specific example: when God chose David to be king, what was the main instruction that he gave Samuel?

Do not consider his appearance or his height . . . the LORD does not look
at the things man looks at. Man looks at the outward appearance, but
God looks at the heart (1 Samuel 16:7).

What was the basic requirement when searching for the ideal person to
lead the people? The answer is impossible to miss: *'Don't look for . . . (but)
look for . . . '* As far as God was concerned, there was something to avoid
and something to search for: avoid the outward, the visible, because
that's secondary, and look for what's inside, in the heart, the **being**.
What a person does has its value, but only when it is the result of a clean
heart, the core of a person's being.

There is another episode in David's life that shows this principle very
clearly because it has to do with his thorn. When the jealous Saul hates
him and David's life enters an extremely dangerous stage, the text says
several times that 'David behaved wisely' (1 Samuel 18:5, 14, 15, AV), to
the extent that 'when Saul saw how wisely he behaved, he was afraid of
him' (1 Samuel 18:15, AV). In the midst of such a turbulent situation, what
stands out is David's character: his attitude, reactions, wisdom, sensitivity, trust in God, respect for 'God's anointed' and his friendship with
Jonathan. There wasn't much David could *do* during his years on the run
in the desert, but it was that very period, apparently purposeless, when
David's character shone more brightly than ever.

My attitudes, reactions and relationships add up to a much more
audible language than my actions or words, however important these
latter may be. They are messages not easily forgotten: a gesture of love
towards our children or spouse in the midst of difficult times; a reaction
showing fortitude in the face of a devastating blow; a peaceful death;
these leave a lasting memory. They are the indelible traces that do not
come from an *act* but from a *life*, what a person *is* rather than what he
does. In fact, after people die they are usually remembered for certain
character traits or particular attitudes: their kindness, generosity or
commitment: 'she was an exemplary wife'; 'he was a loving father'; 'he
was an exceptional friend'. What remains in the memory is their
character – what they were like as people.

Our shining example is our Master. As noted earlier, the most
memorable pages of Christ's life were written in his last days, especially
through his agony when he had to face the most horrible of thorns,
death on a cross.

This is why we agree wholeheartedly with Jean Rostand when he says there is no such thing as a useless life. Every human life, however unproductive or futile it might appear, is a life worth living because, for God, a life's value is not measured by *personal standing* (appearance), but by the *person* (the deepest part of the heart). If the thorn in the flesh has taken away your *doing*, then remember that you still have the more important part, your *being*.

We are only passing through: the priorities of the pilgrim

> So we fix our eyes not on what is seen, but on what is unseen. For what is seen is temporary, but what is unseen is eternal (2 Corinthians 4:18).

'Why are we here, if only to suffer?' is a question asked by many people suffering from cruel thorns in the flesh. Their words echo the perplexity of Job when faced with the apparent meaninglessness of life when his suffering did not go away: 'Does not man have hard service on earth? ... Man born of woman is of few days and full of trouble' (Job 7:1; 14:1).

The answer is important, because it brings us to an essential part of the suffering person's dilemma: the meaning of life. This is not the place to go into this issue in depth but we must emphasize that the meaning of *my life here* depends greatly on my vision of *life after death*. If I think everything ends with death, my existence here will be very frustrating, 'utterly meaningless', as the author of Ecclesiastes puts it. This is a materialistic and atheistic mentality which leads to despair and, in extreme cases, to suicide once suffering comes over the horizon.

But the believer has a pilgrim's vision. It is vital to develop this view of life in order to be able to face the thorns of life. The pilgrim has three attitudes that reflect his or her set of values.

Fixing an eye on eternity: 'looking at what is unseen'

The first characteristic of the pilgrim is that he views this life as something he is passing through, knowing that present sufferings are not worth comparing with the glorious destiny that awaits him. This hope changes the way he looks at life completely, both the good and the bad. It is the perspective that Peter had when he wrote his letter to the expatriate persecuted church, describing them as 'aliens and strangers'. In line with this, Peter argues that suffering is 'for a little while' (1 Peter 1:6), and concludes by encouraging his readers with a beautiful doxology that reminds them of their destiny: 'God . . . called you to his eternal glory in Christ, after you have suffered a little while' (1 Peter 5:10).

It is also the vision that characterized the heroes of faith of whom it is said: 'All these people were still living by faith when they died. They did not receive the things promised; they only saw them and welcomed them from a distance. And they admitted that they were aliens and strangers on earth' (Hebrews 11:13–14).

It is Paul's perspective as well. In 2 Corinthians 4:15 – 5:4 the apostle alternates between allusions to present suffering (vv. 16–17) – an inevitable part of life – and the strength a believer receives as he looks beyond 'to what is eternal'. This is the mentality and the vision of the pilgrim: suffering with his eyes fixed on the goal, knowing that the trial has an end date and longing to be in that better country 'clothed with our heavenly dwelling' (5:4).

Is health the most important thing?

> Though outwardly we are wasting away, yet inwardly we are being renewed day by day (2 Corinthians 4:16).

The pilgrim's second characteristic is his attitude towards the deterioration of his body. Paul has just reminded the Corinthians of the powerful, renewing effect of looking at life from an eternal perspective (v. 18), and this leads him spontaneously to compare the body to a fragile tent ('the tabernacle'), in stark contrast to the one that we shall enjoy in heaven, a solid house not subject to decay: 'Now we know that if the earthly tent we live in is destroyed, we have a building from God, an eternal house in heaven, not built by human hands' (2 Corinthians 5:1).

This being true, the apostle draws an important conclusion regarding priorities: 'Therefore we do not lose heart. Though outwardly we are wasting away, yet inwardly we are being renewed day by day' (4:16).

There is a very relevant practical implication for our subject: the body is not the most important thing in life. We are talking about the body, not health, and this distinction is important. In a biblical sense, as we have already seen, health is a legitimate priority. The problem comes because today health is associated almost exclusively with the body. Being healthy means being physically fit. Health is something you can achieve in a gymnasium or through good dietary habits. It is measured more by the colour of a person's face – tanned features equal good health – or by the size of their muscles.

Clearly, we do not wish to criticize a healthy lifestyle characterized by the best possible habits. This has always been God's will for us, as can be seen in the Ten Commandments and the hygiene rules received from God by the children of Israel. However, today the priority is not so much health, as *the body*. If we reduce health to just its physical dimension, we lose sight of its chief aim: the whole human being. This is why any kind of thorn in the flesh is met with deep rebellion and rejection. In this hedonistic and narcissistic sense, health is not only a priority, but becomes a dangerous idol. Worship of the body has become a massive kind of idolatry in the West, akin to a lay religion with millions of devoted followers.

In such a society, Paul's words highlighting the relative importance of the body's decay are soothing to all those who suffer from thorns that are related to this fragile tent in which we live. It is hardly surprising, then, that the apostle ends this passage sighing for a house not susceptible to pain or suffering of any kind: 'Meanwhile we groan, longing to be clothed with our heavenly dwelling' (2 Corinthians 5:2).

Travelling light: willing to give things up
Thirdly, seeing life as a pilgrim forces us to ditch unnecessary baggage, whether material possessions, incorrect attitudes, inappropriate relationships or any weight that prevents us from 'running with perseverance the race marked out for us' (Hebrews 12:1). The willingness to give things up is a vital requirement for a pilgrim. This is where Lot failed. His life story is that of a man who did not know how to be a pilgrim. Dazzled by appearances, he could not resist the visual attraction of the fertile Jordan plain (Genesis 13:10). He judged and made decisions on what he saw, forgetting that the attitude of the good pilgrim is governed by 'fixing his eyes on what is unseen'. As a result, Lot made the wrong decision, with tragic consequences for his family.

What a contrast with his uncle Abraham! Certainly we must not forget that the patriarch had been tested for many a long year with the thorn of his wife Sarah's barrenness. Abraham passed the test of renouncement with flying colours on several occasions during his pilgrimage. In this episode he was willing to give up material goods. Later, when God asked him to sacrifice his son Isaac (Genesis 22), he showed that his giving spirit was total: he was willing to obey God even though it meant the loss of what was dearest to him. As a good pilgrim, Abraham had learnt that *when God tests, God provides* (Genesis 22:14).

It is not easy to have the vision or the priorities of a pilgrim nowadays because we are swimming against the tide. The pilgrim mentality is not popular, especially in the West, because modern man has become settled from an existential viewpoint, forgetting that he is actually a nomad – passing through – and that, at the most unexpected moment, he will have to strike camp. In general, people in the twenty-first century are tied to life on Earth. They find it annoying to have to think, and even more unwelcome to live, as pilgrims. Unfortunately, they do not realize that by travelling with heavy luggage, worrying about the things of this life, they lose sight of the most important thing: 'Set your minds on things above, not on earthly things' (Colossians 3:2).

Francis of Assisi accurately described the pilgrim mentality in one of his thoughts:

> I need very few things in this life
> and the few things I need
> I need them very little.

The creative value of suffering

> He led you through the vast and dreadful desert . . . He brought you
> water out of hard rock . . . so that in the end it might go well with you
> (Deuteronomy 8:15–16).

A desert full of venomous snakes and scorpions, a thirsty and waterless land: a dreadful place. It would be hard to find a passage that better describes the experience of living with a thorn in the flesh. The crossing of that literal desert by the children of Israel contains a lesson of great symbolic value. We are going to concentrate on one short phrase, but a very significant one for our subject: 'but God brought you water out of hard rock'.

One of the things that has surprised me most in dealing with people suffering from thorns has been the discovery of how fruitful, valuable and useful their lives are. This 'quality of life', as we have already noted, is not measured by *productivity* simply in terms of doing many things. Now I'd like to look at *creativity*, which is the natural complement of a person's *being*, that is, a practical expression of their character.

There is a close relationship between creativity and suffering. We have to use our words carefully here. It is not a question of cause and effect. If it were, we could commit the serious mistake – mentioned earlier – of glorifying suffering and thereby falling into masochism. Let me reiterate that suffering in itself is an evil against which we must fight, a battle in which no quarter should be given. It is not the thorn *per se* that helps us to mature, grow or create, but our response to it. The way we face up to the trial is what determines how much emotional and spiritual benefit we derive from it. The same trial can either sink us or stimulate us. 'Events give us pain or joy, but our growth is determined by our personal response to both, by our inner attitude.'[6]

Let's see, in the first instance, how this phenomenon of creativity in suffering originates.

'Where others see only problems, he sees opportunities'

I first heard these words in reference to a man of God in Spain. He was not a dreamy optimist, a naïve fellow out of touch with reality. Quite the contrary: he had a special gift for finding new opportunities in the worst crisis imaginable. His first question when faced with a difficult situation was not 'What does it stop me doing?', but 'What does it give me the chance to do?' This attitude had a profound effect on how I faced problems or conflicts in my life.

Does everyone have this ability? In a way, yes. God uses trials to perfect our character and to fulfil specific purposes. Suffering also contains, in some mysterious way, an undeniable creative force. There is a close relationship between trials and creativity. Behind the work of many doctors, scientists, musicians and painters, for example, there is often a deep well of personal suffering.

The thorn and creativity: some examples from history

In an interesting book, *Creative Suffering*,[7] the Swiss doctor Paul Tournier makes the observation that a large number of great men in history were orphans. Quoting the work of a colleague, he explains how many of them lost father or mother, or sometimes both, while still young children. He shows how others had been through similar experiences (traumatic divorces, being illegitimate), or had been abandoned by their parents. The author compiled a list of almost 300 well-known influential figures down the centuries who had suffered in this kind of way, from Alexander the Great, Charles V, Cardinal Richelieu, Louis XIV, George Washington, Napoleon and Queen Victoria right down to Hitler, Lenin and Stalin. All of them suffered from some form of emotional deprivation in childhood. Undoubtedly, being an orphan is a thorn that requires adaptation and acceptance.

Yet if we looked only at these famous people, we might think that trials stimulate willpower and nothing more. But this is far from being the case. We find the same phenomenon in many other areas of human activity. Tournier explains how his own experience influenced his vocation for a career in medicine: he lost his father when still only a few months old, and his mother when he was just six; he was then adopted by an uncle. Leonardo da Vinci was an illegitimate child and J. S. Bach an orphan. A study of the biographies of Molière, Stendhal, Baudelaire, Racine, Camus, Georges Sand, Kipling, Dante, Edgar Allan Poe, Tolstoy, Voltaire, Dostoevsky, Alexandre Dumas, Lord Byron, Balzac, Rousseau and Sartre shows that they all suffered some kind of deprivation or disability which was instrumental in stimulating their creative output. In most of the cases mentioned, the experiences involved tragic loss. Others suffered imprisonment or persecution. Alexander Solzhenitsyn and many other writers who were oppressed by the yoke of Communism are a good example of this.

What we have described as affecting the individual also applies to the social sphere. We find a very similar phenomenon when we examine the issue from a collective point of view. The most productive periods in history, in cultural and artistic achievement, have coincided with times of enormous social turbulence and violence. The most extraordinary instance of this is the Renaissance, during which the creative genius of humanity reached what could possibly be described as its greatest heights. Literary and artistic splendour flourished alongside, and amidst, times stained by blood, wars, plagues, injustice and many other forms of immense pain. It is as if human beings need the stimulus of thorns to give of their best, personally and collectively.

The thorn and social sensitivity

Such creativity is, at other times, expressed in terms of *social action*. The ranks of charitable organizations are full of people whose lives are scarred by intense suffering, sometimes to an almost unbearable degree. But here they are, giving of themselves and sharing with others an abundant harvest which the seeds of pain one day sowed in their hearts. Many pioneers and founders of great institutions have suffered at the sharp end of cruel thorns.

A friend of mine developed Alzheimer's disease at the very early age of fifty-two. Both he and his wife were pillars of my local church, committed to the Lord and his work. The thorn of slow and inexorable decline lasted five long years. Unless you have experienced this illness in some close relative, you cannot imagine the brutal impact of the slow deterioration of the person whom you love on the family; it is even harder to take than the deterioration of the body. Following his death, his wife felt a call from the Lord to do something to help families who were in a similar situation. She began to organize local groups to help families who were looking after Alzheimer's patients. Nothing like it existed in the city. In time she helped set up The Barcelona Association of Families with Alzheimer's Sufferers, an organization she chaired for ten years. Only God knows how much good this work did to thousands of people.

Small is beautiful

As you read this, you may well know similar situations of people, anonymous or otherwise, who have reacted to pain with a creative energy that has been hugely beneficial to themselves and others. At this point, however, some readers may feel slightly uneasy. *I'll never be able to do what these people have done; my life is simple and my abilities very limited.* I want to emphasize that a creative use of suffering does not mean that you have to do something great or notable, as in the cases mentioned. You do not need to be a writer or found institutions. Each person, in their own personal desert, can find new ways to be creative, to serve and to work. God can use us in very different ways from those we might have expected or imagined, even in surprising ways. In short, in the midst of the desert we must discover 'the water that God brings out of the rock' because God intends 'to do you good in the end' (Deuteronomy 8:16, ESV). God wants to give meaning to every life, however limited or useless it may appear to human eyes.

Thorns of famous Christians

We shall conclude by looking at some notable examples from the history of the church. It will help you to identify with those whom we normally see as giants of the faith, people of flesh and bone, whose fragility actually brings them much closer to each one of us. They were men and women whom God used greatly, but . . . just like the apostle Paul they were earthen vessels with painful thorns in the flesh. In the words of the great missionary Hudson Taylor, 'all God's giants have been weak people'.[8]

The English psychiatrist Gaius Davies, in his book *Genius, Grief and Grace*,[9] describes eleven cases of famous Christian personalities from the sixteenth to the twentieth century, showing how divine grace used and transformed their weaknesses. It is worth mentioning some of them so that the reader might study their biographies more deeply: Martin Luther, John Bunyan, William Cowper, Lord Shaftesbury, Frances R. Havergal, Amy Carmichael and C. S. Lewis.

Let me give you a glimpse of the problems faced by three of them:

- **John Bunyan** (1628–1688). The author of the very famous book *Pilgrim's Progress* suffered from obsessional blasphemous thoughts which tormented him for several years. It was a symptom of what today is called obsessive compulsive disorder. In his spiritual autobiography *Grace Abundant for the Chief of Sinners* he has left us a magnificent portrait of his thorn: 'The tempter came upon me again and that with a more grievous and dreadful temptation than before. And that was to sell and part with this most blessed Christ, to exchange Him for the things of this life, for anything . . . I was not rid of the temptation not sometimes one hour in many days together, unless when I was asleep . . . Sometimes it would run in my thoughts, not so little as a hundred times together. *Sell him, sell him, sell him, which I may say for whole hours together.*'[10] How encouraging it is to discover God's magnificent grace working through the weakness of this man to produce such a treasure of Christian literature!

- **C. H. Spurgeon** (1834–1892). In this case it was not only one but several thorns. In his early days he struggled with stuttering – what a paradox for the one who later was known as the 'prince of preachers'! Also he occasionally suffered some sort of depressive crisis to such an extent that the only thing he could do was 'escape' to a country house in France, away from everybody and everything, till he recovered. Later he suffered attacks of gout, so painful at times that 'while preaching he had to put one knee on a chair and cling to the pulpit rail'.[11] His ministry was therefore subject to significant limitations; but they were not an obstacle to God's power: He used this man as one of the most outstanding leaders of the church in the nineteenth century.

- **William Cowper** (1731–1800). A great hymn writer, he suffered severe episodes of depression from the age of twenty-one. At thirty-one he had a psychotic breakdown. It was during recovery from this crisis that he became a Christian. 'He was to have five more depressive illnesses before he died at sixty-eight: in between these times he was often amazingly productive as a letter writer and poet.'[12]

Cowper's contribution to the church, and especially its comfort to the suffering person, reaches its climax with his unforgettable hymn 'Light shining out of darkness', also known by its first line: 'God moves in a mysterious way'. This magnificent poem is a summary of some of the main points considered so far in the book. As someone said, 'in this hymn, Cowper has almost created a Christian theodicy which could make sense of his own suffering'.[13] In the first and third verses he admits God's right to keep secrecy, but there is nothing threatening in his divine silence:

> God moves in a mysterious way,
> His wonders to perform;
> He plants His footsteps in the sea,
> and rides upon the storm.

> Judge not the Lord by feeble sense,
> but trust Him for His grace;
> behind a frowning providence
> He hides a smiling face.

In verse two he refers to God as the skilled artificer, as we considered earlier in Joseph's life:

Deep in unfathomable mines
of never-failing skill,
He treasures up His bright designs,
And works His sovereign will.

Persevering along the road: patience and hope

Not only so, but we also rejoice in our sufferings, because we know that
suffering produces perseverance; perseverance, character; and character,
hope. And hope does not disappoint us (Romans 5:3–5).

'If it is difficult to accept, how much more difficult is it to persevere,' said
a mature Christian, blind for thirty years owing to a brain injury. The
effects of grace noted in chapters 4 and 5 are essential to be able to reach
acceptance, but that's not the end of the road. We need to keep fighting,
because the thorn does not go away. Here too we can count on two
precious resources of grace: patience, and hope. It is not enough to
receive grace; we must *persist* in it, as Paul points out in the context of
this passage in Romans: 'We have gained access by faith into this grace in
which we now stand' (Romans 5:2).

Before considering these two final treasures of grace, let's look at an
important idea that Paul emphasizes strongly in these verses (Romans
5:2–3): 'Not only so, but we also rejoice in our sufferings' (v. 3).

Suffering is the only path to glory. This was true for Christ and it will
be true for us. Nevertheless, we must make an important distinction:
Paul is not speaking here about sufferings related to the thorn: the term
'tribulation' (*thlipsis*) refers to the opposition and persecution that the
people of God suffer in a hostile world, suffering specifically related to
the cause of Christ. If we do not make this distinction, we could make
the mistake of thinking that *by* our suffering we contribute to future
glory, an error which has led to such practices as mortification of the
flesh and self-flagellation.

I want to make this clear because the persecuted church was very
much in my mind as I wrote this book. To them, and to all those who
suffer the world's hostility for the sake of the Gospel, Paul directs this
promise: 'Now if we are children [of God], then we are [also] heirs –
heirs of God and co-heirs with Christ, if indeed we share in his sufferings
in order that we might also share in his glory' (Romans 8:17).

Now let's look at two resources that will help us keep going along the right path, operating interdependently, like links in a chain.

Patience

> His purposes will ripen fast,
> unfolding every hour;
> the bud may have a bitter taste,
> but sweet will be the flower.

This is the penultimate verse of Cowper's hymn, and it illustrates the close relationship between patience, waiting for something, and hope: the flower will give its fragrance one day, even though at present it may seem languid and limp.

What 'patience' are we talking about? The term *hypomonē* which Paul uses here means perseverance, as in Hebrews 12:1: 'Let us run with perseverance the race marked out for us.' However, if we limit ourselves to this concept, we have a natural resource which is not specifically related to grace. I can stimulate my capacity for perseverance through merely human methods, whether they be psychological or even Eastern meditative techniques.

The resources of grace, however, go much further than mere human ones: they come from God. That's why the biblical idea of patience is much richer and deeper than mere perseverance. When in Galatians 5:22 it speaks of patience as a fruit of the Spirit, the term is *makrothymia*, which literally means 'greatness of spirit'. The equivalent word in Latin, from which we get our term *longanimity* (meaning 'endurance' or 'fortitude'), refers to a strong spirit that remains firm in adversity. Its opposite, *pusillanimous*, means 'feeble in spirit', whereas *makrothymia* refers to a spirit that does not give up, which does not waver when facing difficult external circumstances. It is exactly the opposite of a cowardly person who 'drowns in a glass of water'.

There is a world of difference between the biblical concept and the popular idea of patience expressed in sentences like this: 'What can be done? There's nothing we can do; just be patient.' This kind of patience is an attitude of resignation when faced with a situation in which you cannot do anything, an attitude born out of, and leading to, fatalism. On the other hand, patience that proceeds from grace does not resign itself but fights. Rather than crumbling in the face of adversity, it gains strength and, instead of being passive, actively looks for solutions.

How do we know that we are progressing in this gift of grace? There is evidence of patience when:

- The person is *self-controlled*. This is one of the essential fruits of patience: it does not react impulsively, as we saw in David's wise behaviour.[14] 'David accepted the fact that he had to live in such hard circumstances. He didn't complain, nor did he resist or try to impress with his piety. He suffered secretly and in silence. Due to this he was deeply hurt. His insides were churned up. His personality was transformed. When the trial ended, David was barely recognizable.' These words refer to the long years on the run from Saul when David had several easy opportunities to get rid of his thorn, i.e. by killing Saul. But David did not do so because he also had the second evidence of patience:

- The person *knows how to wait*. David knew how to bide his time, and was not in a hurry. He let God mark out the hours of his life. God's calendar is not marked in months or years, *chronos*, but by the right moment, the suitable opportunity, *kairos*. A text in James warns us against impatience through an illustration from the world of agriculture: 'Be patient, then, brothers, until the Lord's coming. See how the farmer waits for the land to yield its valuable crop and how patient he is for the autumn and spring rains' (James 5:7). How many of us fall into the trap of haste and are tempted to pick the fruit before it is ripe? The thorn in the flesh means knowing how to wait.

Yet the relationship between patience and hope reaches its climax in its future aspect: the second coming of Christ: 'You too, be patient and stand firm, because the Lord's coming is near' (James 5:8). The kind of patience that comes from grace does not only operate on what is visible; it feeds on a vision of eternal things, especially that of the second coming of the Lord Jesus Christ. This leads us to consider the other great resource of grace that helps us persevere in the struggle with the thorn in the flesh.

Hope

I will live waiting for you, O hope.[15]

I consider that our present sufferings are not worth comparing with the glory that will be revealed in us (Romans 8:18).

Hope is also the result of grace. It is the last of its transforming effects on a person suffering from a trial. Grace helps us cope with the thorn in many ways, but one of the most essential is the fact that it provides us with hope. Only hope can give meaning to life and shine a ray of light into the darkest corners of our existence. The lack of hope is a form of dying while still alive. This is why I want to conclude this book looking higher and further, to the place where faith helps us to glimpse what lies beyond our sight.

The soothing effect of hope while suffering the pricks of the thorn is beautifully expressed in a moving poem by Helen Keller:[16]

O light-bringer of my blindness,
O spirit never far removed!
Ever when the hour of travail deepens,
Thou art near;
Set in my soul like jewels bright
Thy words of holy meaning,
Till death with gentle hand shall lead me
To the Presence I have loved
My torch in darkness here,
My joy eternal there.

Hope for today

As Helen Keller's and Joni Eareckson Tada's lives have shown us, living with hope is always important, but indispensable in times of trial. In *Hope in Times of Crisis*, the Spanish doctor Pedro Laín Entralgo writes about the illustrious Spanish thinker of the last century, Miguel de Unamuno: 'From despair is where real, true hope always springs, and always has sprung.'[17] It is worth mentioning that Unamuno had his own thorn: a son who was ill with hydrocephalus (water on the brain), with all the significant disability that this entails. 'Despair is the ground from which true hope springs, that hope which creates faith that waits.'[18] This 'hope-producing function of despair', as Laín calls it, had already been described by the apostle Peter when he referred to trials as a fiery furnace that purifies our faith (1 Peter 1:7) and strengthens our hope: 'God ... has given us new birth into a living hope through the resurrection of Jesus Christ from the dead, and into an inheritance that can never perish, spoil or fade – kept in heaven for you' (vv. 3–4).

There is, therefore, an immediate application of hope: here and now we wait on God in hope for all the blessings that he has promised to give his children to enable them to cope with the thorn. We wait for his strength each day (Philippians 4:13), his presence (Matthew 28:20; John 14:18), his comfort (Hebrews 4:16), and all the other effects of grace already considered. Paul sums it all up with this encouraging promise: 'And my God will meet all your needs according to his glorious riches in Christ Jesus' (Philippians 4:19).

Hope for the future

> For the grace of God that brings salvation has appeared ... while we wait for the blessed hope – the glorious appearing of our great God and Saviour, Jesus Christ (Titus 2:11, 13).

The dimension in which hope finds its fullest expression is looking to the future. When life is viewed as a journey to a 'better country', it is possible to 'be joyful in hope [and] patient in affliction' (Romans 12:12). This vision of eternity gives us a perspective that soothes the heart torn by pain. This is why hope is inseparable from personal faith in Christ, because it does not come out of nothing nor does it arise spontaneously from the 'ground of despair' (as Laín said). The core of our hope is the future appearance in glory of our Lord Jesus Christ.

As the apostle Peter says, we now have to suffer 'for a little while' (1 Peter 1:6). This expression is sufficiently vague for us not to be able to fix any time limit to it. Perhaps our thorn will be with us for the rest of our life on earth. But, in the drama of life, as in a play, there is a second act, to which we will come very shortly because life is a brief journey, where there will be no thorns of any kind. This is so because God has set a deadline for suffering. If one of the greatest wishes of the suffering person is 'that it all would end soon', this is precisely what Christ did through his incarnation and death. Indeed, the final answer to the enigma of the thorn is not found in any idea or philosophy but in a person, the One who suffered the worst thorn of all: the cross.

The apostle John, in the midst of the thorn of exile and with death just around the corner, describes this hope in a memorable text. It is a passage that has spoken to me very personally over many years and I find it hard to read without feeling moved. These are the best words with which I can finish this book because they are not human, but divine:

> Then I saw a new heaven and a new earth, for the first heaven and the
> first earth had passed away ... there will be no more death or mourning or
> crying or pain, for the old order of things has passed away ... 'I am making
> everything new! ... He who overcomes will inherit all these things and I
> will be his God and he will be my son' (Revelation 21:1, 4–5, 7).

This glorious perspective makes us joyfully respond with the words of William Cowper:[19]

> Ye fearful saints, fresh courage take;
> the clouds ye so much dread
> are big with mercy, and shall break
> in blessings on your head.

Appendix 1: personal testimonies

Ana from Madrid

The thorn

I was expecting my third baby. According to the ultrasound scans and the prenatal tests carried out throughout the pregnancy, everything was fine and the boy would be born healthy. The waiting period before the delivery went fine, and the delivery took place without complications, but when the baby was born, just two or three minutes after seeing its precious little face, I began to sense strongly that something was going wrong. Nobody said anything to us, but the look on the midwife's face and some of her comments were eloquent enough.

Doctors began to arrive and look at the baby and after a few minutes they told us he wasn't well but no explanation of the problem was offered. Finally a paediatrician showed up in the delivery room and informed us that the baby had several malformations that were probably associated with more complications in the internal organs, which was serious, and would require surgical intervention, and he'd know more when he got the results of the tests.

From then on everything became even more complicated. He had an emergency operation in the first twenty-four hours and for a month and a half, after several surgical interventions, his life was hanging from a thread. He didn't respond; the surgical wounds did not heal. He was in neonatal ICU for two weeks and each visit to the ICU was a prelude to the fact that at any moment the worst could happen: he might die. During that time there were moments in which we found ourselves mentally preparing for the burial of our son. On one occasion, after an operation, the surgeon told us: 'Medicine is not an exact science; we don't know what is wrong with your son, only that things are not functioning properly, something is escaping us, his whole organism is failing and I have a bad feeling about it. If you are believers, all that's left is to pray.' My husband asked him: 'Are you telling us that he's going to die?' And the answer was: 'This is what I've been trying to tell you from the start.'

From the time he left hospital at almost two months old until now, our son has been put through surgery eight times. It remains difficult and we continue to worry about how he'll grow up and whether he'll be a normal boy physically. And the obstacle course isn't over yet. He's still awaiting surgery, although his life is not in danger and he lives a normal life.

The first reactions

Right after the birth and for the first few days we experienced a lot of confusion and a feeling of intense suffering. Confusion, because we didn't have enough information, and we were afraid for his life. It was necessary to perform an emergency operation and run many tests, and for me the wait was unbearable. We felt an intense suffering, which affected us to the point of being almost physical, along with the constant idea that the baby was going to die. I remember that I spent several days in constant tears; I was overwhelmed as if I were living in the middle of a nightmare. Owing to the fact that right after delivery he was taken to neonatal ICU, I became totally obsessed with them allowing me to see the baby, to touch him and hug him because I felt that if he died I wouldn't be able to bear the idea of not knowing his little face. My physical recovery after the delivery was set back quite a bit, which I imagine was due to my sadness: I wanted to disappear and die, or wake up and see that it was only a bad dream.

From the start I had a terrible feeling of **guilt** that didn't leave me until months later. Even today, I sometimes have to battle with this idea. To think that I might have done something wrong during the pregnancy, that I might have taken something I wasn't supposed to, that I might have done something that I shouldn't have ... I felt that I had to ask forgiveness for not having a healthy son and, in fact, at the beginning I did just that. Between the tears I would say to my family: 'I'm sorry.' Everybody, the doctors, my family, would tell me that it wasn't my fault. But, despite the evidence, that thought tortured me very much.

If nobody is at fault, then **why?** This question, which arose from the depths of my pain, was very present during the first few months. Why did it have to be *my* son, why me, why a baby ... ? All the **'whys'** were left unanswered. Silence. Today, I have accepted that silence. But I no longer ask myself why. I've learned not to do it. I know there is no answer.

Departing from the hospital without my son, leaving him in a serious state and coming home without him in my arms, produced in me a feeling of total emptiness, and from there the sadness went on to be intense, brutal and devastating. Seeing his things, his bedroom, expressing milk every three hours in order to keep up my milk supply just to pour it down the drain . . . I truly wanted to die; I couldn't sleep; I wasn't even able to rest for a minute and I scared myself thinking of terrible things like going to the kitchen, taking a knife and committing suicide. Once, this feeling, this thought, was so intense that I became afraid because I really thought I'd go through with it. I was beside myself and would constantly wake my husband up and cry with him. I scared myself. The idea and the thought of wanting to die were constant. Not improving, I had to get medical help in order to get some sleep and also for the depression. As soon as I did get some sleep, I improved a little bit, but the intense suffering lasted for almost two months.

When the major crisis was over, we brought home the baby, who was now two months old. During these past three years, we have returned to the hospital numerous times to continue with the surgical interventions. There have been other operations in which things have looked quite bad and have become complicated in surgery or where things didn't turn out right and it was necessary to intervene once again . . . it even seemed like the norm for our son that things would not work out the first time. Despite the calm and joy of having our son with us, feelings of anger, distress and enormous sadness arose within me that my little son should have to suffer so much.

The spiritual battle: prayer, the key to our experience

At first, in the midst of my stupor, I only asked God 'why' repeatedly, but I don't think that it was a question looking for an answer. It was a clamour. It was the verbal manifestation of my inner sadness and my falling to pieces. It was the expression of a totally broken heart.

After the first few days, when I could finally think with a bit of clarity, I began to pray intensely. I prayed alone and with my husband. I prayed at home and at the hospital. I prayed asking for help and for support, not asking for any explanation. I simply knew that the only one who could do anything for my son was God. I remember that we would go to visit our son in the neonatal ICU and we would pray while holding his hand. I remember that it was clear to me that I had to pray to God asking him to heal my son. I simply felt that I had to do it. I had to ask God time and time again to have mercy on us and let us keep our son. Like David with Bathsheba's son, pray and pray and wait for God to do something: in this case we asked that he should heal our son.

I remember that one day in the midst of intense suffering I said to my father: 'Dad, don't pray for God to do his will and for us to accept it. Pray for God to do a miracle and heal Daniel, and not take him away.' Later I said to him humbly: 'Please, Dad, pray fervently that he should live. If he dies, then we'll pray to God to be able to accept it.'

I especially remember the day that we were told his life was draining away, and that we should prepare ourselves because he was going to die. After crying all afternoon, my husband and I finally reacted and told each other that we must pray and pray. Together with our family and a lot of other people, we asked God to perform a miracle. I trusted in God that he could do it. I would tell him during those days of struggle: 'God, grant him his life.' God's performing a miracle and saving Daniel was experienced by me as a victory for his love and mercy. God showed tender compassion towards me and my husband and, instead of taking away this treasure, he left it for us to enjoy. Three years have gone by, and we are still going through trials, but each day I feel and each day I remember that having Daniel is a gift.

During the following months, it's been much of the same. There have been many difficult moments and God has always comforted us. Prayer has been the means. It continues to be the means. A sincere prayer, from the midst of our spiritual poverty and lack of understanding.

Also, when we've had moments in which we lacked sufficient strength even to pray, others have done it for us. Support from family, church members and friends has been very important to us. We have felt it vividly. I have always told them that they have been like the 'hands of God', his direct touch and caress. I know that God has 'held' us using the hands, shoulders and embraces of many people we love.

Acceptance

Acceptance for me has been difficult. During the first few months I learned that there is no answer to my 'whys'. Only silence. But not an icy silence, rather a silence based on the trust that God really KNOWS what is happening. Quite frankly, I do not understand the purpose of what has happened to us. I don't understand, and that's that. I thought that maybe someday I would discover a reason instead of asking why. From all this suffering we have learned much. We have grown in humility, in compassion, in thankfulness, but we have also learned some very hard things, like the harsh feelings of pain, sadness and the shadow of death. Easy answers like: 'God has allowed it to happen as a test of your faith' make me sick. If I thought like that, I would stop believing in a tyrannical God who uses the suffering of the helpless for who knows what spiritual victory. Others have told us that it's for the glory of God, and I have the same reaction. I don't believe it; my son hasn't been born with malformations for anybody's glory. For him it has been and will be the cause of much suffering. I don't understand God in that way. For that reason, acceptance for me has a lot of silence, trusting and believing that there is no answer, and thinking of God and of Jesus looking at me tenderly in the eyes saying 'I'm here, with you; Daniel's life is precious to me.'

Sources of help

The company of my husband who has gone through and is going through a similar process has helped me to accept this new situation. Being able to talk to him about the contradictory thoughts and feelings has been and is very liberating. It's important for me to verbalize and express myself without the fear of being judged or getting lectured. Simply having someone who'll listen to me and let me cry and express my anguish has made it possible for me to begin rebuilding myself in the new situation that we face.

My family has also been vital. My parents, my brother, my sister-in-law, my brother-in-law and some of my closest friends have been essential in this process. I always remember a phrase that my brother said to me a few days after Daniel was born, because it helps me to orient myself: 'Ana, what's coming up is going to be like a very long obstacle course.' That vision helped me to visualize my situation better than many other explanations. I know that we have begun the race, we've got through the largest obstacles, and some day (I don't know when) we'll reach the finish line.

The act of feeling profound gratitude towards God for leaving Daniel with us makes the path of acceptance much easier.

Adapting to a new situation

The practical help we received from my family was fundamental. It was quite difficult, and still is even today, to organize the family when we have hospital stays and post-operative care. Their constant support and dedication is incredible.

Putting things into perspective also helped me. It all depends on how you look at a problem and, after thinking that we were going to lose Daniel, having him with us at home, even with his many medical problems, for me is like a balm. A change in values, realizing that having a healthy child is not the norm, it's a blessing. In hospital we learned a lot by seeing situations much more serious than that of our son. Now I know how to value what's important. I worry much less about things in general.

The most difficult part for me

I have a hard time accepting the emotional wear and tear that this has meant for me and my marriage. Two years practically tied to the hospital and keeping the situation as normal as possible, trying to get through it ... I think that during those two years we've aged at least ten. It's difficult for me to accept that it takes its toll on us, but that's the way it is.

Grace that is sufficient

For me, throughout these years, God's grace has been in knowing and feeling that always and at every moment God has not abandoned us; that God's success is not seen in the external blessings (good health, a home, healthy children...) but rather in those of the soul (peace, confidence, contentment).

Our weakness has also been extreme, and God's grace enormous. The worse off we have been, the closer we have felt the hand of God. I wouldn't choose this. If someone told me about this, I would ask that it should not happen to us. But it has, and God helps us every day and especially when we go through difficult times at the hospital.

As I said before, I have learned many positive things. I feel that I am now a person who has a more authentic outlook on life, more real. I have grown a lot in compassion and mercy, because I have felt that God has shown them immeasurably to me. I have learned that, regarding children, few things are worth worrying about, and what I took for granted before, I now consider a gift. I have learned to show solidarity from the heart with people who suffer. I have learned that it is better to live life one day at a time, because life, as Forrest Gump's mother would say, is like a box of chocolates. You taste one, and you may like it, but another you don't like at all . . . and you have to eat it anyway.

I've also learned some difficult things: you can lose your joy and your hopes, and if you don't take care you can become sceptical, cynical, unbelieving . . . because you don't believe in the apparently happy setting. It's an experience that takes its toll on you and places you at a crossroads: either you continue forward trying to see things in another light and focus on things in a positive way, or by inertia you continue to be bitter, distressed and without hope.

How my values have changed due to the thorn

I appreciate the present, the day to day, much more. Faced with the uncertainty of what may happen, I try to live each day at a time, and that's all.

I have become much more humble. I don't pretend to prove anything to anybody, or give lessons about anything. Feeling the thorn, the weakness . . . has made me lose all pretensions if I had any, and adjust my expectations as a mother and a person.

It has made me regain and relive Christian values which are felt so deeply when one gives oneself to Christ: grace, mercy, compassion, and trust in God. I'm less demanding. I understand human fragility better. Before, I judged others a little, but now I don't judge them at all. The burden of suffering that many people carry is immense.

Jose and Marta

This moving testimony was written by Jose and Marta, from Menorca, Spain. They are the parents of Marc, a sixteen-year-old boy suffering from cerebral palsy. Written in the first person, it puts into words what Marc himself is unable to express.

My name is Marc. I was born on Friday 20 April 1990, just over fourteen months after my parents' wedding. At that time they were twenty-eight years old, and I was their first child. For nine months I heard them talking excitedly about my coming birth, about how happy the prospect made them. I remember their reaction when they saw me in a scan, just a few weeks after my life had begun, arranged because of a car accident my mother had had. I remember my father saying something about understanding now what it really meant to feel for a child. My mum and dad prepared everything meticulously for my arrival: antenatal classes, my future room decorated and furnished so that I would feel as comfortable as possible in it. Everything was beautiful. Then one morning my mother was making the bed when her heart skipped a beat. For a moment, she later said to my dad, she felt that something was wrong. But they just put it down to nerves, logical, of course, as the day drew nearer.

When the day arrived my mother went to hospital, and someone had to wake up my dad, who was on call there, at around 7.00 in the morning. He thought he was being called to attend to a patient, as he's a doctor, but the attendant's voice got him out of bed more quickly than usual. Mum's waters had broken on the day that the delivery was due. From that moment on, for the next nine or ten hours, the contractions had not let her rest for a single moment: hyperdynamic uterine contractions, I think is what they call them. At about 4.00 in the afternoon, the channel through which I was going to arrive had been prepared and I was taken to the delivery room. Twenty minutes later the contractions came to an end and my heart started beating more slowly. I had to be got out of there very quickly, but for some reason someone decided to delay the moment of delivery and, when the cold metal tongs were clasped around my head, with no time to put my mum to sleep, I wasn't conscious of anything any more. I just heard someone saying that I wasn't breathing when I was born, and that my heart wasn't beating either.

While they were dealing with the damage that the forceps had caused my mother, my father, getting more and more agitated, watched the doctors' desperate efforts to revive me. He knew that it wouldn't be possible that night to put me in the room that they had been so lovingly preparing for me. He was praying with all his heart. About half an hour later he saw me move one of my toes, and a little after that they were able to stop all those strange massage manoeuvres all over my little four-kilogram body.

At that time there was no such thing as a CT scanner (a machine used for seeing right inside a body) on Menorca, the island where I was born, and the director of the hospital told my father that we would have to go to Mallorca to get this done. During the journey they had to tie my arms with bandages as I didn't stop moving and trying to tear off the drip feed that they had attached to me. My father and grandfather were pleased. I was moving my body as if nothing strange had happened that afternoon.

I was taken into the paediatric ICU, and my family went home until the next day, Saturday. They wouldn't be doing the test until the following Monday. Everything seemed to be going well, and there was no urgency.

On Saturday everything seemed to be going fine, too, but when my father arrived on Sunday, confident that all would be well, I wasn't there to see him. They told him that that night I had had a series of convulsions and they had had to give me an injection in the back, and had found blood in the fluid that surrounds the central nervous system. They suspected a subarachnoid haemorrhage, blood between the two layers that cover the brain – the meninges. This was confirmed that same day by the CT scan, which was brought forward by a day. It was too early to know for sure, but I wasn't moving as I had been before, and I had gone into a coma. My father didn't want to say anything to my mother, who still hadn't recovered from the delivery in the hospital on Menorca, although she noticed something in his voice when they spoke on the phone, and she couldn't help worrying. Something must be wrong. My father's anguish was unbearable. He never stopped praying for me, but the news was getting worse.

On Monday night, the day before my mother arrived, my father prayed in a different way. He told God that he didn't agree with what we were going through, but that he was prepared to let him do his will with me, even if he didn't like it, because he had learned that God's will was always more perfect than his own. Mum arrived on Tuesday. She had not been allowed to see me since those few seconds when she had me on her belly just after they had wrenched me, flaccid and pale, from her body. She was still in a wheelchair, recovering from the injuries that the traumatic delivery had caused her. They told me that she said I was beautiful. I suppose I must have been, because everyone who saw me just after I was born kept talking about how beautiful I was. I don't have any photos of that time, though, as no one took any until I was a month old.

That night my father went to bed torn apart with anguish, as he had done every night since I was born. He was praying relentlessly, when suddenly he was overwhelmed by an indescribable peace. He was able to sleep as he hadn't done for several nights. The next day, however, he didn't feel any different. The anguish was back again, and he barely remembered the experience of the night before. My father asked God if he was trying to tell him something. Was the peace that he had felt some kind of sign that his son was going to be healed? As he is a rational type of person, he immediately asked God, if that interpretation was the right one, to cause someone else to have the same experience that he had had. Perhaps, after all, it was a kind of mechanism whereby he could escape from reality, or a projection of his intense desire that everything would be well. He decided not to say anything about it to anyone, and just to wait.

The next day my mother woke very early to come and see me through the glass that separated us: there I was, in the incubator, surrounded by tubes and wires; there she was, in the visitors' corridor. It was at that moment that she too was overcome by a deep sense of security; it was as if someone were whispering words to her that filled her with peace: 'He'll be all right; everything's fine, I have him in my hands.' Later, my father arrived. When Mum explained this to him she remembered his prayer of the night before: that someone would have the same experience, and that he would hear of it. They talked about it together, and from that moment on an indescribable peace filled their hearts. Day after day the doctors came with bad news about my condition; each time he went to my mother and told her. But the news did not affect them. 'The peace of God which passes all understanding' – I have heard my father reading this text from the pulpit – filled their hearts. They had done nothing, they had not used any kind of self-control technique, nor suggestion, but they had peace.

The next day my father missed the bus that he usually took to the church in the Calle Murillo, in Palma. There they were praying for me and for a child of three, the son of some friends of my parents, who had thrown himself from a third-floor flat shortly before I was born and seemed to be recovering. He decided to go on foot, which meant that he arrived after the service had already started. They asked him to sit in the last pew, where there was a free space. At the end of the service the lady who had been sitting next to my father introduced herself. She had heard about what had happened to us and wanted to meet all three of us. She said she had a message from the Lord for my parents. They arranged a meeting the following day in the hospital. She told them that she had been praying for many years for a son of hers who had a cerebral lesion, which caused him to have fits. At eighteen years old the boy's fits ended. The mother asked the doctor who had been caring for him to arrange for a CT scan, to see what condition his brain was in. The lesions had disappeared. 'You will be praying for your son for many years, but the Lord has heard your prayers,' she told them. They were dumbfounded, and thanked the lady for her interest in them, and, like Mary, 'they pondered those things in their own heart' (Luke 2:19).

The weeks passed, and I gradually got better and better, and the time came to have a routine CT scan. There was permanent brain damage. What could not be foreseen was whether my intelligence and mobility, etc., would be affected. Thirty-five days after my birth, at last it was time for me to go home.

My parents had become hopeful, but what they were about to face back home was not as pleasant as they had imagined it would be. I had never been outside hospital. The noises in the street, and the darkness of night-time, were a source of terror for me, and I cried and cried. Hours and hours they spent cradling me in their arms. Hours and hours learning how to feed me. Nevertheless, they were beginning to see the trauma of the events surrounding my birth as a nightmare that had passed. Perhaps it was for that reason that when they took me, at the age of three months, for my first appointment with the neuro-paediatrician, and he told them – in a manner that was distinctly lacking in sensitivity – that I showed all the symptoms of cerebral palsy, my father broke down. He ran out of the surgery weeping. He tried to find a place to hide along the corridors of the hospital, unable to control his sobbing. My mother had to call a taxi to take us to the airport, to get a flight back to Menorca. My dad didn't stop crying until we'd practically boarded the plane. When we got back home, he was furious. Had God not broken and moulded him enough already when he was younger? I never heard the details, I guess my mother knows, but he had been through a really bad time during his last years at university. Why couldn't he have been struck down instead of me? I had my whole life in front of me, while he had already had a chance to see at least something of life. I don't remember how long it took him to calm down. All I know is that never again since that day have I seen him so broken, so angry. My mother kept calm. That's what they are like: when my dad is crushed, my mother helps him to come through it, and vice versa.

The first years were marked by frequent nights of prayer, pleading with God that I would be healed. My parents' church, and my own, is not a 'charismatic' church. But it is a church that believes that God intervenes in the affairs of human beings, whether it be in the control that he exercises over creation and history through his providential care, or through the kind of specific miracles that Scripture records.

During the second summer of my life my mother had a crisis. My sister Irene had just been born. My father was working overtime at the hospital. During the night I would often cry for hours on end. I remember that when I was beginning to fall asleep in the arms of my mother or father I would suddenly get some kind of 'scare' which would make me wake up suddenly and cry at the top of my voice. And this would go on for hours. At that time my mother was on leave from work; she was a teacher, and she was devoting all her time to caring for us. For that reason it was usually she who had to put up with my 'screaming fits', as they used to call them. During that summer my mother would be on the terrace of my grandparents' house near the beach in the small hours of the morning. She would wrestle with the Lord in prayer. Why did everyone else seem so contented while she, who had tried to be faithful to God, had to deal with this?

The battle lasted a full year until, at the beginning of the following autumn, she was able to summon the strength to say to God that she wanted to thank him for the situation she was in, even though she didn't like it. From that moment on she was able to accept her circumstances. She stopped comparing herself with other people. She no longer needed me to be healed. She felt special, chosen by God to look after me.

I have mentioned one of my two sisters, Irene. She was born fifteen months after me. When my parents heard that they were to have another baby they were very frightened. I was barely six months old, and everything was so recent. Logically, the doctors took all the precautions they could, and when the slightest doubt arose they performed a caesarean section. The unplanned arrival of my sister was a source of enormous blessing to my parents. During the first year of my life, they had been comparing my development with that of other babies of the same age. I couldn't sit up, I couldn't crawl, there was no sign of 'my first word', I couldn't even hold up my head. As the doctors had never ventured to forecast what my final state would be, this process of comparison between my development and that of other babies was tormenting. In every aspect of my growth I wasn't 'arriving on time'. In fact, as far as most things were concerned, I would never arrive. For this reason the birth of my sister was a source of concern for my parents. Would this torment caused by comparing me with healthy children be even greater now that they would have a healthy child at home?

That did not happen. Miraculously, with the birth of my sister all the comparisons came to an end. I was I. Irene was Irene. Each of us would have our own life, and our own personal development.

Two years after Irene, Maria, my other sister, was born. On the night of her birth, my dad was with my mother in the hospital. He was sitting in an armchair, feeling sad. He was asking God how long our situation was going to go on. I was not getting any better. At that moment he heard these words of a song by Paquita Patiño through the earphones of his Walkman™:

There will be times when your tears
Will not let you see
What the Father wants to do within you;
But one day you will wake up
And see that the night has passed,
That the pain had to be,
So Christ could be formed within you.

A deep peace came over him. 'Until Christ would be formed within you.' There was a purpose and a time. He never again prayed for my healing. Indeed, my parents have been reproached for that choice by many a well-meaning brother. 'We don't pray for Marc as we used to.' They usually point out that God has heard their prayer. 'If Marc is to be healed, he will be, even if we don't remind God of his condition every day. If not, our insistence is not going to make God change his mind.' If I am still as I am, it is not because of any lack of faith on the part of my parents. I remember once when my father came back home after a prayer meeting and he came into my room to see if 'the miracle' had happened. God acts in response to faith, but faith does not oblige him to act in any particular way. Above all else, there is his will, which does not always coincide with our desires.

One memory that I have from that time is of going along the street with two prams, one of them Maria's and the other mine, with Irene, at two years old, walking alongside. That was a good time. I think that lots of people must have thought our parents were mad. Three children in three years, and one of them with cerebral palsy! But they always say that if they had had to plan the births of my two sisters, they would never have had the courage to go through with it. The girls have been a blessing from God for them, and for me. I love watching them arrive home, and hearing them talk to me. Now we don't play as much as we used to. They have got older and they have their own lives, but we still often have moments when they play with me, and talk to me, and we laugh together. I recognize them and I can tell them apart. When Maria sees that I am having trouble getting to sleep at night she comes and reads me a story. And it works, because I fall asleep immediately. Now they are big girls, and they can stay with me alone when our mum and dad need to do something, or go out somewhere together. But God has also given Mum and Dad the blessing of having fantastic parents, my grandparents. They are always attentive to my needs, and always ready to help with the day-to-day tasks of looking after me.

We had six or seven really hard years. At night I had terrible problems sleeping. I never managed to get off until about two in the morning, and very often I would wake up several times during the night. Fortunately my two sisters were very different in that sense. I don't think my parents could have coped with a second or third 'cry-baby', even if they'd been only a tenth as bad as I was. In fact, during my worst period, my sister Irene had the immense virtue of scarcely needing any attention at all during the night. In fact she would cry if anyone tried to help her to sleep or took her up in their arms too often. I think it was God who was seeing to that.

Between the ages of seven and eleven was a good time. I liked going for walks and outings. We even went to the Port Aventura theme park once as a family. Then, just as I was entering pre-adolescence, other problems started. My hands started to become deformed around the wrists and my feet around the ankles, due to the excessive tone my muscles had because of my condition. That wasn't too worrying. It just meant that people would stare at me more when we were walking in the street. The worst thing was when I started to develop scoliosis, a curving of my spine towards one side. The doctors said it was normal in children like me during the period of fastest growth. The result was that I became progressively unable to remain seated in my pram. This had serious consequences for our regular family routine. We couldn't go away together any more. I spent most of the time lying on a sofa or on an armchair. Someone always had to be with me. This loss of autonomy really upset my parents. Everything seemed to be getting worse. The curvature of my spine often made it difficult for me to breathe. Doubt, fear of the future, fear regarding my life expectancy became, and still are, a source of terrible anguish for my family.

When this happens they have two resources that they rely on. The first one is their past experience with God. When they were young, at university, they had to learn about God's providence. They learnt that God was interested personally in their lives. As a matter of fact they had had many opportunities to see that not a single hair of our head falls to the ground without our Father's permission (indeed in Dad's case God is very generous with his permission as far as his hair is concerned!). For that reason they never doubted that God had not just got distracted during those fateful first minutes that determined my future. They also learnt that God never arrives late, and he never arrives too early either. He is always punctual. Some years ago my father preached a series of sermons on the book of Job. When he got to chapter 38 he found what has been his mainstay during these last years. When Job interrogates God about the origin of and the reason for suffering, the Lord does not answer his questions. Instead he confronts Job with the reality of his providence in the past, and he also confronts him with the fact that this same providence governs the circumstances that Job is passing through.

'Who is this that darkens my counsel
　　with words without knowledge?'
(Job 38:2)

Job has to humble himself before God. He has no right to know all the answers, but he has been transformed by God. He has acknowledged God's universal rule, his sovereignty, and his right not to give explanations at every point and in every situation. Then Job is restored, as happened to my dad when he surrendered to whatever God would decide to do with regard to me just a few days after my birth. I have not been healed. I don't know, and my parents don't know, whether I ever will be, or whether God simply wanted to give them peace at that time, and they interpreted from that peace more than God wanted them to take from it. Or maybe they didn't understand the timing of the promise.

The book of Hebrews records the fact that many of the people who received the promise from the Lord in the Old Testament 'were still living by faith when they died. They did not receive the things promised; they only saw them and welcomed them from a distance. And they admitted that they were aliens and strangers on earth' (Hebrews 11:13). The truth is that when someone is capable of recognizing their weakness, their lack of resources, then they are ready to depend on God absolutely. It is then and only then that the power of God is made perfect in their weakness (2 Corinthians 12:7–10). Without this acknowledgement of our weakness we always face the temptation of thinking we can 'lend God a hand'. When we do acknowledge it, then all that remains for us to do is depend on God, and wait for a manifestation of his power. What happens next depends on nothing but the all-powerful action of God, with no contribution whatsoever on our part.

The second resource is what the Word of God has been teaching them little by little. Apart from what I have been commenting on up to now, I have heard that the letter to the Romans says about Abraham that he 'in hope believed and so became the father of many nations, just as it had been said to him, "So shall your offspring be." Without weakening in his faith, he faced the fact that his body was as good as dead – since he was about a hundred years old – and that Sarah's womb was also dead. Yet he did not waver through unbelief regarding the promise of God, but was strengthened in his faith and gave glory to God, being fully persuaded that God had power to do what he had promised. This is why "it was credited to him as righteousness"' (Romans 4:18–22).

Sarah's womb was drier than my bones are deformed and my muscles contracted. The body of Christ was dead and the power of God raised it up again. I know, for my parents have told me, that one day we will all be raised up with a new, glorious body. My hands, my feet and my spine will not be deformed then. I will be able to speak rather than only move my head and smile (that's something I do very well – they tell me I'm a real conqueror!). And my mother will have her dream come true of seeing God face to face, as Marcos Vidal says in a song with that title:

Only one word, only one prayer,
When I enter into your presence, O Lord,
I don't care at which place at the table you ask me to sit down,
Or the colour of my crown, if there's one for me to wear.
Only one word, if I still have a voice
And if I get a chance to say it in your presence;
I don't want to ask you questions, just one prayer,
And if I can be alone with you to say it, all the better . . .

Only let me see you face to face, and lose myself like a child in
   your gaze
And let time stand still and no one say a word
Because I'll be looking on my Master face to face;
Let my memories all disappear as I look into your face,
I want to love you in silence, without words,
And let time stand still, and no one say a word,
Only let me look at you, face to face.
Only one word, only one prayer
When I enter your presence, O Lord,
I don't care at which place at the table you ask me to sit down,
Or the colour of my crown, if there's one for me to wear . . .

Only let me look at you, face to face, though I fall and melt
   to nothing in your gaze,
Defeated, from the ground, trembling and breathless,
I will still not cease to look at you, my Master;
When I fall at your feet, on my knees,
Let me weep, let me cling to your wounds,
Let time stand still, and let no one keep me away
For it's the moment I've been waiting for, all my life.

My mother says she will probably not need answers, that merely looking at him will be enough for her, that then she will understand everything, and she'll be able to cry and cry and cry . . . Mum, I want to tell you that I believe the Lord will let you cry, but then he will take you in his arms and wipe every tear from your eyes, for there will be no more sickness, nor death, nor sorrow, nor groaning nor pain. He will make all things new, and he will reward you for all the years that you've spent serving him. Especially for the time you spend caring for me.

Zeena: My faith in God gives me strength

Refugee in orbit for seven years

When Zeena Rassam, a forty-year-old Christian chemical engineer from Baghdad, married her husband, Salam, at the Mariam al-Athraa church in the Iraqi capital in 1997, she had no idea that on their tenth wedding anniversary they would be living in an asylum centre surrounded by barbed wire in a remote

Scandinavian country. Three years after their wedding Zeena and Salam were forced to leave Iraq because of their Christian faith.

Today Zeena, Salam and their eight-year-old daughter, Meena, are among the thousands of Iraqi Christians who are paying a high price for their Christian faith – in this case the price of living with fear, anxiety and an uncertain future as failed asylum seekers awaiting deportation. Having been denied asylum in Denmark, Zeena and Salam are among the 600 Iraqi asylum seekers that Denmark hopes soon to send back to Iraq by force. According to the Danish immigration authorities it is safe for them to return to their country despite the fact that hundreds of civilians are killed every month in the mounting political, religious and ethnic violence. The fact that Zeena and Salam were explicitly threatened because of their Christian faith is not considered sufficient to obtain refugee status. Here Zeena tells her story.

What gives me strength is my faith in God. I have prayed every day all my life. I learned to pray as a child, but at that time I did not know what I was saying. Now I know. God has become much more real to me since we left Iraq.

In Iraq we had a good life. My husband, Salam, owned a shop and a car rental firm, and I was a lecturer at a technical university in Baghdad. We had a young daughter and lived in a big house with my parents-in-law. On Sundays we went to church as a family. Then all of a sudden our life was turned upside down. One day two men came to our house with a recording they had secretly made of something my husband had said about Saddam Hussein. They were Muslims and did not like us because we were Christians. They demanded that we pay money or they would kill my husband. They wanted 3,000 dollars, a very large sum to us. We were very scared. With the help of family and friends we managed to pay the money. But after two weeks they came back demanding more. Then we knew that we had to leave. We had often seen what happened to people who were reported to be against Saddam Hussein. We had a young child and did not want to take any risks.

Within two weeks we had sold our shop, firm and car. It was all done in deepest secrecy. Then we left. We drove through the desert to Jordan during the night. It was very dangerous, but there was no alternative route. We knew that at any time we could be stopped by armed gunmen. The journey took seventeen hours. All the time we prayed to God for protection. I had never been so afraid in all my life. Twice we were stopped and searched. They even checked our daughter's nappy. But both times they let us go. As we did not have enough money for all of us to continue to Europe, we decided that Salam should go on ahead while I waited in Jordan with our daughter. After twenty-five days of travelling by plane and lorry and hidden in a container, he arrived in Denmark in the autumn of 2000. We both breathed a sigh of relief. We thought that after a few months or at most a year he would get asylum so that he could find a job and pay for us to join him.

But things turned out very differently. In the end Salam waited three-and-a-half years before he heard anything from the Danish immigration authorities – and then his application for asylum was rejected. During that time he lived in four different asylum centres where he was not allowed to work and provide for himself or for us. Then he was transferred to a special centre for failed asylum seekers. Three years later he is still there. Today he is forty-eight years old and has not been working for seven years.

When Salam left for Denmark I stayed behind in Jordan illegally. As I had no residence permit I could not work, and my daughter could not go to school. With the money Salam had left with me I rented a small flat. On the other side of the street was a church. I could not stay in my room all day so we went there because it was so near. It was an evangelical church with only about fifty people. But they were absolutely fantastic. I had many questions, and they listened to me and prayed for me. In the church I heard God speaking to me and telling me to trust him. The pastor often came to see me and explain the Bible to me. When we were ill the pastor and his wife helped us. I had no money to see a doctor or buy medicine. We went to the church several times a week. On Wednesdays we met to pray, and on Saturdays I taught Bible stories to the children. They still pray for me, phone me and send e-mails.

During those years alone in Jordan my Christian faith became much stronger than it had been in Iraq. I suffered much and experienced all kinds of anxiety and fear. But now I know why I had to stay in Jordan for five years. I feel that God wanted me to get to know him better. Those years were God's answer to my prayer. In Jordan I learned to pray directly to God because my need was so great.

Then after five years I was deported to Iraq with my daughter. It all happened very quickly. I had been desperate to get a job as I had been totally dependent on others for so long. Eventually I had found a job illegally. But after two weeks the police came. They took my passport and all our things and left us at the Iraqi border with a five-year ban on re-entry to Jordan. Just like that. We had no money. Nothing. An Iraqi family who had also been deported took us to Baghdad in their car. Here we stayed with Christian friends. I had no family left in Iraq whom I could turn to.

At first I thought that we might be able to build a new life in Iraq now that Saddam Hussein was not there. It was June 2005 – two years after the US-led invasion. Perhaps the situation was better now, so that Salam could come back and join us. But I soon discovered that Christians were not safe in Iraq.

Because of what I had experienced with God in Jordan the church was very important to me. I started going to an Assyrian church near the house where we were staying. I went two or three times a week. In the time of Saddam Hussein it was not dangerous to go to church. But now it was very different. When I went to church I had to wear a *hijab* so that only my face was visible. Many Muslims thought that Christians supported the US-led occupation because we had the same religion as the coalition forces. Sometimes we found leaflets in the streets or in the garden telling Christians to leave Baghdad or pay with our lives. There were slogans on walls that read 'You must become a Muslim or we will kill you'. Today, Christian friends in Baghdad tell me that they have heard similar messages from some minarets: 'You must become a Muslim, or pay money, or leave within three days.'

One day two men with long beards came to talk to the owner of the house where I was staying with my daughter. 'We know that you have a guest living with you. We have seen her go to church. If she doesn't leave this district we will kill her and kidnap her daughter,' they said. They told my host that I had preached to Muslim people, as sometimes Muslims had come to our church and asked questions about the Christian faith. I had answered their questions. I did not know why they came. At first I thought that they wanted to know the difference between Christianity and Islam, but looking back I suppose they were trying to catch me out.

After the two men had left I was really frightened. I made sure that my daughter did not leave the house, and went to see my pastor. But the same people had also threatened him, so he told me not to come to the church any more – it was too dangerous. When I later needed his help with getting a passport, I jumped over the wall to our neighbour's garden and left through their house, hiding myself in my *hijab* so that only my eyes were visible. The pastor was very understanding and helped me. I also got money from my mother in the States, which she had borrowed from family and friends. I had no home and nothing I could sell. I needed 10,000 dollars to pay an agent to take us to Europe. Today they say that the same journey costs 30,000 dollars because the situation in Iraq is much worse now.

I wanted to go to Denmark, where Salam was, and at least then we could be together. But Salam did not want me to travel in this way. He had tried it himself and knew that many die. So I did not tell him that we would try to come. We just left. The journey took eight days. First we went by taxi to Syria. Then we hid in a van that took us to Turkey. From there we continued up through Europe in another van. We sat huddled together in the dark and stopped only at night. I have no idea where we have been. I just prayed all the time. Sometimes I thought we were not going to make it. My daughter had a temperature and was very afraid. 'Why are we here?' I cried out to God. But I knew I just had to go on. The day before we left Iraq I had prayed much to God. Was this the right thing to do? I felt he had answered that this was the time. And we were lucky. We survived. Nothing happened to us, and by the grace of God we were not stopped.

I cannot describe what it was like to meet my husband again after five years. I could not feel anything even though this was the very day that we had been longing for and dreaming of for so long. Since Salam had left we had mostly communicated by text message as it was cheaper than talking on the phone. My daughter did not recognize her father. He was a complete stranger to her. She was only two years old when he left Jordan, and now she was seven. In the beginning she cried a lot and had nightmares about the journey and the bombs in Iraq that had exploded every day. Now she is better and has started playing like other children.

After seven years we still have no idea what the future holds. Sometimes we feel that we are hostages in a political game. Many days we feel that our life here is marginal and meaningless. We are just waiting, but what for? We have nothing to do. We can only sit and worry about what is going to happen to us. Three times a day we go to the centre cafeteria for our meals. We are not allowed to cook our own food. When the cafeteria opens we have to be hungry and to eat the food while it is there. If we miss a meal we have to wait until the next one is served. I try to read some chemistry books that I borrowed from our Danish friends, as I don't want to lose all that I have learned. But sometimes it is hard to concentrate. Twice a week we have to report to the police. Every time they ask us the same question: 'When will you go back to Iraq?' And we repeat the same answer: 'We are not going back because it is not safe.'

But I refuse to give up hope. I continue to dream of the day when my daughter will be allowed to go to school like other children, and when Salam and I will be allowed to work. A day must come when we don't have to fear the future. I still believe that God will give us a future. He has helped me so many times in the past. Now I am asking him to help us again.

I am not bitter. Somewhere deep inside me I have peace. Life has taught me to be patient and to trust in God. Not everything depends on external circumstances.

Perhaps we will have to stay in this asylum centre for the next ten years. We don't know. Only God knows. We cannot imagine living here for ever without being allowed to work or learn anything new. It is especially hard not to be able to give our daughter a future. Sometimes she asks why we have to stay here. She knows that we had problems in Iraq; she can still remember. But she cannot understand why we cannot have our own home like the Danish people.

I pray and pray. Does God hear me? I know I must not ask that question. At least I am safe here, and we are together as a family. My situation is much better than many people's. Even if Denmark will not allow us to live a normal life, this asylum centre is still better than the ongoing violence and targeted killings of Christians in Iraq.

As an Iraqi my life would probably have been a lot easier if I had not been a Christian. But I would not want to be anything else. I am thankful to God that I am a Christian. If I did not have my faith, I am sure I would be much more stressed and fearful. When I ask why I am here in this situation, I feel that God says, 'Wait, this is not the time for you.' I often read the Psalms in the Old Testament. Here God tells me not to be afraid. He will be with us. His rod and his staff will comfort us. It is as if he is speaking directly to me.

Today we know many Danish people through the church. They are very kind to us. We can feel that their hearts are with us. They are our lifeline. Many Danish people pray for us. We are not alone.

In spite of all our worries and anxiety I still try to smile and laugh. My Danish friends say that I am optimistic by nature. I am sure that nothing can continue for ever. Change must come one way or another. I have faith in God that he is not going to leave us suffering. I am sure that God has something good for us. He has a plan for us. Knowing this gives me strength to face tomorrow.

A personal testimony

This is a true story. It appears as anonymous since the person who shares it asked us not to disclose her identity.

I woke up on Wednesday 7 June 1989 and got ready to take my three children, aged thirteen, eleven and nine, to school. My right arm had some peculiar sensations and a feeling of great coldness, and I realized it was not functioning as it ought to and was losing strength. I bundled the children into the car, dropped them off at school and went straight to the doctor's.

The doctor could see that I was panicking and hyperventilating so he thought it best if I lay down in one of the surgery rooms and he would keep me under observation. As time went on I became almost completely paralysed. I was anxious but very aware of God's peace. A lot of what happened was a blur, but I remember quite clearly being calm and sensing God's presence in the midst of turmoil. They sat me in a chair but I fell out of it, as I had become completely paralysed. I was frightened by what was happening to me. A lumbar puncture did not reveal the cause so they sent me to a hospital in Hampstead where they had a very good neurological department.

There they did a myelogram, for which they had to inject me with a dye and do a succession of X-rays. By now my whole body was paralysed and each time they moved me into a different position to be X-rayed it was agony. It took a few weeks for them to decide that I had had what is called a thrombosis of the anterior spinal artery, which in layman's terms is a blood clot in the C4 (fourth vertebra down from the top) region of my neck, which had damaged my spinal cord. They did not know what had caused it. I was also in spinal shock, which normally lasts about six weeks, and any recovery occurs during that time. My bowels and bladder had been affected. Then there was a scare that my breathing would be affected too and I was sent to the intensive therapy unit as I might have had to go on a ventilator – but mercifully my breathing started to improve. I was kept in ITU for a few days just to make sure. Everyone else around me was dying.

My left leg started to recover and I could move it. They moved me back to the ward, where I was prodded with sharp pins to test my body's reactions. My right leg started to move but my arms could hardly move at all. My left arm had lost the use of the triceps muscle and was stuck bent up; I couldn't straighten it. My hands were both clenched. They put splints on them to try to straighten them out. I had been lying flat for a long time so when the physiotherapists came to sit me up I felt faint and saw black dots before my eyes. Eventually, two of them got me to stand by holding me either side. My head fell like a sack of potatoes and I had a job to hold it up. They started wheeling me to the gym but although my bladder and bowel had been paralysed they now started to work, but I had no control, and felt humiliated. My hands and arms weren't working properly so I couldn't feed myself, so I had a rota of people to feed me. I felt pretty hopeless and useless. Every day the effort of having a bath and washing my hair made me pass out.

I was then transferred to another hospital for rehabilitation. I thought, 'Now I'm going to get better and get all my functions back.' I was so sure that God could not leave me like this – could he?

The occupational therapist fitted a spoon to a splint so I could learn to feed myself. Gradually, my left hand improved enough for me to hold the handle, but it was so heavy I could barely lift it.

After six months I could walk a limited distance. My left arm was still folded up at the elbow joint. My right arm just hung with the hand curled up.

I finally came home in a wheelchair. My family, friends and church had been wonderful, especially my husband. His mother, a seventy-one-year-old widow, had moved in and looked after my children. She was marvellous, but my nine-year-old daughter had got used to her taking my place and addressed all her questions to Grandma. I was home but felt I had lost my role as mother. I couldn't cook or do anything I had previously been able to do. Mother eventually returned to her home. I was in charge again but could hardly dress myself. I had nurses coming in to wash and dress me, and had to watch a home help do all the things I should be doing to run the house.

My first reactions

When it first happened and I was in the Royal Free Hospital I had feelings of numbness and being afraid of what was happening to me. Later I experienced frustration and anger – why had the rug been pulled from under my feet? I hated not being there for the children, especially my daughter. I had feelings of anxiety for the future. I didn't feel life was worth living like this. I felt worthless and useless and very depressed.

The spiritual struggle: pleading with God

At first, God gave me great peace and I was convinced that he would heal me and not leave me as I was. It helped that I encountered so many Christians, even a Christian nurse praying over me in tongues! Every night I went to bed expecting to wake up in the morning healed. Why had God allowed this to happen? I realized that, although outwardly I appeared to be doing all the right things as a Christian, I knew in my heart that I was not walking close to him and was backslidden; my quiet times had slipped. I did feel a sense of guilt. What hurt me most was not being at home with my family. I pleaded with God to heal me – I said to him that I could never be happy unless I was healed. I was quite happy (well, I would endure the suffering) as long as in the end I could be back to normal, doing what I had always done. I was prepared to suffer for a time while God taught me a lesson as long as I was all right in the end physically.

What helped me most

Certainly the counsellor I was sent to was no help: I was pretty depressed when I went in to see him and much worse when I came out. The greatest help was my husband, always cheerful and helpful but spiritually solid. Reminding me that God was sovereign and, even though I could see no purpose in what had happened to me, God *did* have a purpose. Romans 8 verse 28. I wasn't even considering how awful it was for him; I selfishly just thought how it affected me! He never complained once about having done a full day's work, then visiting me and finding time to spend with the children. Many friends didn't know how to react. I'm sure I would have said something stupid myself. The best help was a friend who visited me, saw my anguish and cried with me, not saying anything – a bit like Job's comforters before they opened their mouths! Knowing people were praying was a great comfort.

Letters and cards and visitors – just knowing I was loved helped. I was frustrated that I was not able to do anything, so I thought that I was useless to God. It was pointed out to me that God was interested not so much in what I could do but in just who I *was* as a person. I was also helped by advice such as 'Take one day at a time' and 'Achieve one goal a day'.

Facing a different life: acceptance and adaptation

When I arrived home disabled, faced with a different life from what I had before, I could see only blackness and no light at the end of the tunnel. I didn't want to live like that and wanted to die. I just pleaded with God to take this feeling away. It took me two long years to realize and accept the reality that although I had made some recovery I was never going to be completely healed. This was my new reality: I couldn't walk that far, my arms had limited movement, bowel and bladder were not working properly, causing many problems, and I couldn't cook, clean or dress myself. This was going to be It and I wasn't going to get any better.

Slowly, bits of sunlight peeped through the darkness. I had felt bereaved in losing the bits of my body that didn't work. God had always been there and got me through, even though at my bleakest times he seemed far away, therefore I knew he would see me through battling with my disability. Once I realized that I had to accept what had happened to me and that he was not going to heal me, I had peace. I had accepted that what had happened to me was God's sovereign will and I slowly started to see how great God is. As I have said already, he gave me a great husband, who encouraged me in everything. He adapted my car and taught me to drive again. I made deep friendships with Christians I didn't know very well before and had the joy of praying with them. One friend in particular came faithfully every week to stretch my hand and put it through passive movements, and continues to this day. I have made a deep friendship with a non-Christian lady I met in hospital who was paralysed from the neck down, whom I seek to witness to.

Some blessings coming from my experience

I have learned so much from what has happened to me. God has certainly been able to use me to witness to other disabled people who are not Christians. I said that I would never be happy unless I was healed, but God changed all that and, although it would be good to be back as I was, he has given me his strength to cope with being disabled. He has also given me contentment. I can see with hindsight many blessings that have come from my experience. He is all that I need to help me through each day, with all its difficulties. His grace is sufficient.

My real values in life now

Each day is precious and I don't take it for granted. Material things don't mean anything any more. Running around doing things is not important. The real value in life is having a close relationship with the Lord, keeping close to him every day. My relationship with Jesus is much more precious to me now than health and material possessions.

Dennis and Nanette

I have been a Type 1 diabetic since 1957, when I was almost five years old. They diagnosed my brain tumour in Madrid in May 1999. My wife, Nanette, and I had been serving as missionaries in Spain since 1982. It had been an uphill battle for us, with my diabetes, one daughter with severe asthma, another with Attention Deficit Disorder, and a car accident in 1985 that left Nanette with improperly treated neck injuries, resulting in chronic pain. And that was just the physical portion of the battle!

In the three years prior to my tumour, Nanette's cervical spine had been operated on three times in an attempt to correct the damage and relieve her pain. After each bout of surgery she spent several months in a neck brace, twenty-four hours a day, and had to sleep only face up and not bend over, lean, turn her head, twist, etc., while on her feet. She became very good at picking things up with her toes! When I called her at our apartment in Madrid from what we thought was an appointment to check problems with my vision and said, 'Hi, hon, I have a brain tumour,' she thought I was kidding.

'What? That's really not funny.' Not funny at all, but true.

That was Monday; the specialist wanted to operate on my brain on Wednesday. Our experience with medical care in Spain being what it was, we took the MRI films of my brain to our family doctor the following day for his advice. The tumour was plainly visible even to the uneducated eye. He told us to be back in America and in an operating theatre within ten days. Our youngest daughter was in high school in Madrid.

'How about a month? Our daughter needs to finish more of the school year.'

'No, ten days,' said the doctor.

'Well, could it be two weeks, then?'

'I don't think you understand. You have ten days and no more. Dennis must be in surgery having the tumour removed no later than that.'

We returned to our apartment in a daze, packed our suitcases, called family in America and friends in Madrid, and asked my mom to find us a neurosurgeon who could do the surgery in ten days. Our older daughter was already in college in California and our younger daughter was pulled out of school in Madrid to return to California with us.

Nanette and I had been singing and performing together since 1973, and at the time of the tumour diagnosis we were working on our fourth recording. Our good friend, sound engineer and producer, Adolfo, also worked part-time for Delta Airlines. He put us on the stand-by list immediately. By Thursday we were at the airport boarding a plane, with two friends holding my elbows, carrying me to the plane. The doctor was right: I was deteriorating so quickly that I couldn't even get to the plane by myself. There was much discussion among the crew and with Adolfo but we didn't pay that much attention. We were just relieved that all three of us and our dog were on that plane and bound for a hospital in California. Later on, Adolfo told us that they had not been going to allow us to depart on the flight. We had no letter from the doctor and, indeed, I would have been deemed too ill to fly. Adolfo told them that I was just very nervous about the flight! Not untrue, but not the whole truth, and we were glad we didn't find out about it until afterwards.

On Friday afternoon, we, with our mothers, Nanette's sister and our younger daughter, April, were in the neurosurgeon's office in Newport Beach. My mom had seen his name on his office door at the hospital and called for an appointment, explaining our situation. He spent over six hours explaining everything about the tumour and the surgery. He answered all our questions. He made drawings of everything he was going to do. He was meticulous, compassionate and straightforward – an excellent physician in every sense. He took only patients he wanted to take, and he would take me. He also promised to take in payment whatever our medical insurance gave him, and to make sure that the hospital did the same.

On exactly the tenth day, I was in the operating theatre at St Joseph's

Hospital for ten hours while the neurosurgeon carefully removed the tumour from my brain. The lobby was full of friends and family accompanying Nanette, Megan and April and praying with them all day. When the surgery was finished, Dr Malkasian came out to the lobby and spent another hour and a half explaining everything to them, with drawings, and answering everyone's questions. Then he took Nanette's hand and said, 'Let's go see your husband.' He did not know at that point whether I would be able to talk or swallow after the surgery. When they leaned over me and I said, 'Hi, hon,' he was thrilled. My right side was paralysed but my words were still intelligible.

Sixteen days in intensive care followed, with intravenous feeding to keep my blood sugar stable. Nanette lived between my bedside and the waiting room, where she attended to the visitors who came to check on me. Friends came by and took her for a meal or brought food to her, knowing she wouldn't eat otherwise. A piece was missing from the back of my skull and a drain came out of the top of my head. Tubes stuck out of my neck and arms and my face drooped like that of a person who had had a stroke. My right arm and leg were useless, hanging like dead branches.

When I was released from hospital I left on a Zimmer frame. We rented a house close by from loving friends, and for more than six weeks I had to return on weekdays to the hospital for radiation treatment. This made me sick and my blood sugar levels were wildly unstable. I still had the drain in my head and they were monitoring the amount of swelling inside my brain. The strain on Nanette was incredible. Imagine that your spouse's brain is traumatized, he is diabetic, vomiting and convulsing, and will be in an irreversible coma if you can't get sugar into his blood-stream. And you have to get him to his daily radiation treatment, which is what is causing this and will make it happen all over again tomorrow.

This part of the journey was agonizing. Only the grace of God sustained us through the prayers of family and friends. When it was over, I learned to walk without the Zimmer, although with a limp and a shuffle, and I learned to write with my left hand, and even to draw and paint a little again. I couldn't sing or play musical instruments any more.

When Megan got married a year later, I walked her down the aisle and gave her away. As we stood in the same doorway in which Nanette had stood with her dad twenty-five years earlier, ready to walk down the aisle towards the groom, the wedding guests' eyes filled with tears as they watched this clumsy dad cross the sanctuary threshold with the beautiful bride on his lame arm. They were witnessing in that moment the answer to prayer, theirs and mine, that I would live long enough to walk my daughters down the aisle at their weddings. I performed the ceremony, including giving Eric and Megan communion in their first act as husband and wife. What a profoundly joyful day it was! The bride and groom surprised us at the reception with a twenty-fifth anniversary cake and we were happy and grateful to be able to celebrate on their wedding day. They cut their cake according to the Spanish tradition, with a sword brought from Spain. Nanette had added her own touch by having the blade engraved with their names and wedding date.

A few months later, we were ecstatic when Dr Malkasian told us that we could return to Spain. He had given me a life expectancy of four to six years, since my type of brain tumour (ependymoma) is 100% recurring. April would be able to return to her school in Madrid for her senior year and graduate with her class. Megan and Eric were settling into married life. Nanette and I could go back to our life and ministry in Spain for as long as I could cope. God was merciful and allowed us to discover little by little how idealistic that was.

The part of my ministry that I did on the computer I could still manage with one finger of my left hand. However, the seminary in Madrid where I taught classes decided that they did not want me to continue. Nanette and I disagreed with this decision and took it up with the founder, with whom we were long-time friends and collaborators in ministry. We felt that the students had deeper lessons to learn about Christian living from a professor who had persevered in the face of trials and come back to teach them, giving out of his store of knowledge. We were grieved that the seminary did not agree and considered my changed physical appearance too great a distraction. Nanette was angry, feeling that this communicated to the students a message that was in direct opposition to what true, mature Christian values should be. However, the decision was made.

We returned to the recording studio with the goal of finishing the CD that had been started three years earlier. Nanette shuffled the songs and arrangements around in order to preserve the guitar and vocal tracks that I had recorded. As Adolfo is also a first-class guitarist, he added guitar tracks to fill in where I had left off.

We also returned to our beloved church and to Madrid Gospel Choir. We were welcomed back to both with open, loving arms. I couldn't do much but it seemed that just showing up encouraged people. I was the mainstay of the tenor section of the choir before and I could barely open my mouth now, but they loved to have me there with them. They made sure I got up and down the risers and kept me from falling off when we were all swaying or jumping to the beat. We all had a good laugh in one song where we had to turn right round together. I made it back round to face the front a long time after everyone else, but I made it.

During the ensuing months it became clear to us that when April graduated from high school the best thing for us to do, indeed what God would have us do, would be to return to America and be near our family for whatever earthly time God gave me. Megan and Eric were in Southern California, April would be there, our parents were there; Nanette's sister and our home church were there. We knew it was the right thing to do but it was also the hardest thing to do. The CD continued to evolve and became our farewell to Spain. Nanette cried right through the last six months.

We had to limit our cargo to what would fit in a forty-foot container and our suitcases. Much of our furniture was sold but we could not part from antiques we had bought in Spain, so they went into the container. Amazingly, the shipment of CDs arrived from the factory the day the container arrived at our house to be loaded. We left several boxes out for distribution in Spain before we left and the rest were sent with our belongings. The next Sunday we presented the CD at our church. People took copies and asked Nanette to sign them. She was there for hours, signing CDs with tears streaming down her face. This was her goodbye to our church, to the language, culture and ministry in which we had invested our lives, and to our beloved Spanish friends.

Part of the plan in returning to California was for Nanette to find a job and a home there before I got to a critical stage at which it would have to be done under much more stressful conditions. She had returned to college and finished her bachelor's degree during the years that we were going through our surgeries. God provided her job and the house and I was able to claim disability allowance. Every missionary has to discern for him- or herself what to do in debilitating circumstances, but when it became clear that we could not continue our ministry work full-time, we were convinced that it was not right for us to live off the financial support of our donors. Even so, our team is so amazing that we still have a small group of people who continue to support us faithfully every month.

In 2002 Megan and Eric had our first grandchild, John Mark, and we were crazy about him. I had lived long enough to become a grandfather!

Having struggled through tumultuous high-school years, April made unwise choices. She was angry with God and punished herself and those of us who loved her by her actions. She became pregnant by a young man who was not a Christian and who did not want the responsibility of fatherhood. We were heartbroken. Our second grandson was born in 2003 and our grief at giving him up was outweighed only by our gratitude that April chose to give him in adoption to a wonderful Christian couple who could not have children. This way, Jaden would have a father and a mother to raise him and give him a stable Christian home. His adoptive parents would keep in touch with April and us; we would know how he was and see him from time to time. We watched April place her baby boy in their arms and whisper through her tears, 'I'm doing this because I love you.' It was the most generous and unselfish act we had ever witnessed.

Marian Rose was born to Eric and Megan in 2004, our first granddaughter. She was round all over with black hair and eyes. She captivated us from the first moment we saw her and I suppose will always have us wrapped round her little finger.

By the spring of 2005, my six years were up. People asked me how I was, and my happy, surprised answer was always, 'I'm still here!' I thought I would go from the operating table to heaven, then from the four-year point to heaven, sometime between four and six years to heaven, but still to be here after the doctor said I'd be gone . . . !

Nanette and I had been attending the Hispanic congregation at our home church for a couple of years and participating in the worship team. I had got one finger of my right hand to the point at which I could play one string of the bass. That's all you need for bass strings. My left hand could play on the neck just fine. I couldn't play as well as before but the worship team valued me as a member and an example. Nanette sang, played keyboards and taught vocals.

I volunteered in our church office every Wednesday morning, caring for people who came in to ask for help. The church also had a list of people with cancer who had asked for prayer. I started calling everyone on the list every Wednesday. If they didn't answer the phone I left a message so they knew someone had called and was praying for them. We also had a group that met in one of the cancer patients' homes each week to talk, pray and share information.

People make odd assumptions about cancer patients. Nanette and I learned to smile and nod graciously in response to shallow, ignorant comments. We talked together about how interesting it was that I had terminal and chronic degenerative illnesses with no pain, while she had not known a pain-free day or night since September 2005, and how all that affected us. Praying together became the most treasured part of our marriage.

I was approached by a friend of a friend with an online school and asked to teach apologetics online in Spain. I was happy to agree to do that since it was one of my areas of expertise in ministry. I had done a lot of work on cults while in Spain and produced resources in Spanish, of which there had been a woeful lack for Spanish-speaking Christians all over the world. With an open door to focus on it again, I want to get as much done as possible in the time I have left.

The autumn of 2005 brought the fulfilment of another dream. I walked April to her groom's side at Laguna Beach. Josh was in the Navy and home on leave, deploying for Bahrain in two weeks. We were all in wartime wedding mode. Josh was wearing his dress blues. It was an intimate family group gathered for a very meaningful ceremony. This was the man God had intended for April, ever since they had met in junior high. They had reconnected in the spring of 2005, fallen in love again as adults, and wanted God's blessing as they sealed their marriage covenant before Josh left for the Middle East. It was a happy, happy day, complete with another wedding cake to cut with the Spanish sword.

Josh came home on leave six months later. He was able to stay for a month before returning to duty in Bahrain. He and April conceived our fourth grandchild during that month.

With my annual MRI scan that summer came the news that I had a new tumour in another part of my brain and new lesions in my spine. The brain tumour was so close to the optic nerves that surgery wasn't possible. We opted for stereotactic radiation on that tumour and radiation of the entire spinal cord for the others. Treatment had to be done at the University of California, Los Angeles (UCLA), where they had the machine for the stereotactic radiation and the skill to use it. Depending on traffic, that meant driving for at least an hour and a half each way every day. I couldn't drive myself because the treatment made me sick, dizzy and unable to stand. It knocked me off my feet. Family and friends formed teams to drive me back and forth as Nanette couldn't afford to take that much time off work. Megan was there when I was brought home to make sure I made it to the bed to lie down. She kept an eye on me until Nanette got home from work. My diabetes had to be taken into consideration: if I got sick and my blood sugar plummeted, one person had to be able to take emergency care of that while the other one handled the car. People took time off work to drive me. They helped pay for the fuel for our trips. Our church paid for fuel and for us to stay for several weeks at a residence near UCLA in order to relieve some of the stress of the whole ordeal. Nanette did stay for one week with me there and April, with Josh far away, stayed for a couple of weeks. She was a tremendous help as she cared for me, and sometimes, with her pregnancy, we were just nauseous and exhausted together! We ate an awful lot of soup. My skin was burned, my throat was raw, and I was very wobbly on my feet and thinner than when I had been a skinny teenager. It was a long, long two months. My family suffered watching me suffer and was tense with worry about my diabetes. What a relief when the treatment was over! It was weeks before I could eat normally again.

In the meantime, Josh and April got their orders for his next posting. They would be moving together to the Pacific Missile Range in Kauai. Lydia Faith would probably be born in Hawaii! My next goal was to meet her. We had to pray Josh safely home and help April to get ready to move with him. He got home just six days before they left for Kauai. Three weeks after they arrived, Lydia was born. Nanette flew over the day before and was there to keep her unbroken record of not missing the labour and delivery of any of her grandchildren. April gave birth quickly and the baby was perfect. In a couple of weeks, I will be travelling to Kauai to meet Lydia and visit Josh and April.

My follow-up MRI scan after the radiation treatment shows that all the tumours that were treated have remained the same and new ones have shown up on my lumbar spine. This is not good news. Surgery and radiation are no longer options. Chemotherapy is an option, with about a 5–10% effectiveness rate on this type of cancer cell. We are meeting Dr Malkasian next week to discuss whether, because of my diabetes, going through the treatment is worth it. I trust God. He has granted my desires to see my girls married, hold my grandchildren, and even minister in unexpected ways. I would like to live longer, but, whatever God chooses, may his will be done.

Appendix 2: types of thorn

This outline is just an illustrative reference point, and is not intended to be a comprehensive list of every possible thorn. It is just a small sample that mainly reflects my own experience as a psychiatrist and as a lay leader/elder in a church for more than thirty years. The list is intended to broaden the types of thorn mentioned in chapter 1, especially those related to disease. Any situation of chronic or recurring suffering having the features described could be added here by the reader.

Chronic physical illnesses

These can be:

- Degenerative: multiple sclerosis, Parkinson's disease, muscular diseases (dystrophies), other neurological diseases
- Incapacitating: disorders causing sight or hearing loss, certain forms of diabetes, renal insufficiency necessitating dialysis, chronic heart conditions, serious rheumatological diseases that hinder mobility, etc.
- Recurring in crisis form: epilepsy, malaria
- Infectious: HIV (AIDS virus), hepatitis B and C, tuberculosis.

In many cases these diseases are degenerative, incapacitating and recurring at the same time.

Chronic psychological illnesses

- Serious and recurring depression
- Obsessive disorders with intrusive (undesired) thoughts
- Schizophrenia and other psychoses
- Personality disorders: antisocial, borderline and others
- Different types of addiction, including alcoholism, compulsive gambling and sexual addiction (the thorn here affecting more the family than the patient, who is often unaware of the problem or reluctant to solve it).

Appendix 3: glossary of medical terms

Brucellosis – a bacterial disease chiefly affecting cattle and causing intermittent bouts of fever.

CT scan – computerized tomography scan that uses X-rays to build a picture of the inside of the body.

Ependymoma – a tumour of the cells supporting the nerve cells in the brain and spinal cord.

MRI scan – magnetic resonance imaging scan, which is similar to a CT scan but uses magnetism instead of X-rays to build up a detailed picture of areas of the body.

Hemiplegia – paralysis of one side of the body.

Hydrocephalus – excess fluid in the brain.

Myelogram – an X-ray examination used to detect abnormalities of the spine, spinal cord and surrounding areas.

Psychotropic drugs – Drugs that affect a person's mental state.

Self-concept – The mental image or perception that one has of oneself.

Stereotactic radiation – the use of a computer-guided system to aim highly focused beams of radiation directly into brain tumours.

Tetraplegia (also quadriplegia) – paralysis of all four limbs.

Notes

Chapter 1: Paul's thorn and ours: identifying the enemy

1 Anonymous poem quoted by Albert Schweitzer in his biography *Albert Schweitzer, la vida de un hombre bueno*, Jean Pierhal, Editorial Noguer, Barcelona, 1955, p. 75.

2 Today the estimated percentage of patients surviving cancer in Spain is 64%. Source: interview with Dr José Ramón Germá, director of the Department of Oncology, General Hospital of Catalunya, *La Vanguardia*, 15 March 2007, p. 80.

3 200 million people is the estimated number of Christians suffering persecution today and 350 million are exposed to some form of discrimination or restriction of their freedom, according to the Religious Freedom Commission of the World Evangelical Alliance.

4 One book that covers this subject is *Their Blood Cries Out – The Untold Story of Persecution Against Christians in the Modern World*, Paul Marshall, Word Publishing, 1997.

5 John Calvin, *Calvin's Commentaries, Corinthians Vol. II*, Eerdmans, Michigan, 1948, p. 377.

6 William Barclay, *The Letters to the Corinthians*, Saint Andrew Press, Scotland, 1961, p. 287.

7 John Stott, *Calling Christian Leaders*, Inter-Varsity Press, Leicester, 2002, pp. 54–55.

8 In some diseases of the cornea, small water-filled cysts are formed in a recurrent way and become very painful, leading to a state of physical and emotional exhaustion.

9 F. F. Bruce, *Paul, Apostle of the Free Spirit*, Paternoster Press, Exeter, 1997, p. 136.

10 Jean-Paul Sartre, *Nausea*, trans. Lloyd Alexander, New York: New Directions Publishing, 1964, p. 170.

11 To readers interested in exploring this subject we suggest: *Where is God When it Hurts?*, Philip Yancey, Zondervan, 1990; *Where is God in a Messed-up World?*, Roger Carswell, Inter-Varsity Press, Leicester, 2006, and *How Long, O Lord?*, D. Carson, Inter-Varsity Press, Leicester, 2006.

12 Joni Eareckson Tada became tetraplegic as a teenager after a diving accident. Her life and her books, reflecting an unshakeable faith in God, have had a deep impact on an entire generation of believers around the world. I heartily recommend her books as an unfailing source of encouragement.

13 Joni Eareckson Tada, *Secret Strength for Those Who Search*, Multnomah Press, 1988, p. 13.

14 Quoted by John Stott, *The Cross of Christ*, Inter-Varsity Press, Leicester, p. 333.

15 Doug Herman, *What Good is God?*, Baker Books, Michigan, 2002, p. 93.

16 John Stott, ibid., p. 335.

17 Dietrich Bonhoeffer, *Letters and Papers*, p. 361.

18 Don Carson, *How Long, O Lord?: Reflections on Suffering and Evil*, Inter-Varsity Press, Leicester, 2nd edn 2006.

19 Joni Eareckson Tada, ibid., author's note.

Chapter 2: The thorn hurts: wrestling with God and oneself

1 John Calvin, *Calvin's Commentaries, Corinthians*, Volume II, Eerdmans, Grand Rapids, 1948, p. 374.

2 The verb 'to buffet' – *kolaphizō* – that Paul uses can also be translated as 'to maltreat, treat with violence'.

3 Recognized as such in the *Diagnostic and Statistical Manual of Mental Disorders*, 4th edn (DSM-IV).

4 Ibid., Editorial Masson, p. 639.

5 Robert Shuman, *The Psychology of Chronic Illness*, Basic Books, New York, 1996. This is how the author entitles chapter five of his book.

6 Shakespeare in his play *Richard II* (II.ii.14), quoted by Shuman, ibid., p. 83.

7 Those interested in exploring this subject further may read the book *Tracing the Rainbow: Walking through Loss and Bereavement*, Pablo Martinez and Ali Hull, Spring Harvest Publishing Division, 2004.

8 In psychiatry this is called Acute Stress Reaction, cf. section F 43.0 of the *Diagnostic and Statistical Manual of Mental Disorders*. It is considered to be an Anxiety Disorder.

9 Eleonore van Haaften, *A Refuge for My Heart: Trusting God Even When Things Go Wrong*, Christian Focus Publications, Fearn, Ross-shire, GB, 2001, p. 44. This book is an excellent complement to our topic, as it takes the reader into the lives of Naomi, Ruth, Joseph, Leah and David to discover how they dealt with their personal circumstances of suffering.

10 Roger Hurding, *Coping With Illness*, Hodder and Stoughton, 1988, p. 38. Dr Hurding's life and work is a remarkable example of how God can use a chronic disease to accomplish his positive purposes.

11 This is a chronic lung disease that often causes death when the patient is quite young.

12 Written on a picture at the Carthusian Monastery of Santa María de Tiana, Barcelona.

13 Most authors today support the idea that anxiety is a multidimensional problem with a mixture of inherited proneness (the temperamental or constitutional factor), learning, environmental disturbances and current factors. Since this is not an academic book, we deliberately omit references.

14 In some cases, when the level of anxiety is high, it is properly considered a psychiatric disturbance called Generalized or Widespread Anxiety Disorder.

15 This is how two doctors, Holmes and Rahe, described it when they developed a method for evaluating these changes and for measuring the person's consequent stress level. As a result, they created what is known as the Social Readjustment Rating Scale.

16 For a further study on the subject of stress, I warmly recommend the book *Honourably Wounded: Stress Among Christian Workers*, Monarch Books, London, 2001, by Marjory F. Foyle, a medical doctor and psychiatrist with thirty years of experience as a medical missionary.

17 For further reading on this subject, I recommend *I'm Not Supposed to Feel Like This*, Chris Williams et al., Hodder and Stoughton, London, 2002, which is a Christian self-help approach to depression and anxiety based mainly on the cognitive therapy that I will explain in chapter 3.

18 Philip Yancey, *Prayer, Does It Make Any Difference?*, Hodder and Stoughton, London, 2006, p. 229.

19 John Calvin, ibid., p. 376.

20 Os Guinness, *In Two Minds: The Dilemma of Doubt and How to Resolve It*, Inter-Varsity Press, USA, 1976, p. 13.

21 Quoted by José M. Martínez, *Tu vida cristiana* (Your Christian Life), Clie 1982, p. 30.

22 For a deeper understanding of this vital aspect of the topic, see chapter 12 ('The Comfort of Providence: Learning to Trust') of Don Carson's book *How Long, O Lord?*, Inter-Varsity Press, Leicester, 2006.

23 Charles Swindoll, *Perfect Trust*, J. Countryman Ed., USA, 2000, p. 13.

Chapter 3: Acceptance: the key weapon for defeating the enemy

1 The authorship of this so-called *Serenity Prayer* has been under discussion for a long time. Most evidence, however, points to Reinhold Niebuhr, the German theologian, as its author. This is how it was first acknowledged by the magazine *Alcoholics Anonymous Grapevine*, January 1950, pp. 6–7. The authorship of Niebuhr is also recognized in *Bartlett's Familiar Quotations*, 16th edn, edited by Justin Kaplan, 1992, p. 684.

2 Original title in French *Syllogismes de l'amertume*, Editions Gallimard, 1952.

3 Ibid., Spanish edition, Emil Cioran, *Silogismos de la amargura*, Editorial Laia, Barcelona, 1986, p. 103.

4 Adam J. Jackson, *Secrets of Abundant Happiness*, p. 37.

5 For further reading on the importance of positive attitudes when you face rough times, I recommend Viktor Frankl's work. Although he does not write from a Christian viewpoint, this Jewish Austrian psychoanalyst, a survivor of the Nazi concentration camps, has produced a number of helpful books. For our subject, his *Man's Search for Meaning* is an excellent contribution.

6 To those readers interested in exploring this subject further, we recommend the books: *Les Vilains Petits Canards (The Ugly Ducklings), The Whispering of Ghosts: Trauma and Resilience*, and *The Love that Heals*, by Boris Cyrulnik.

7 Death by crucifixion was slow, lasting 18–20 hours, and was considered the most heinous of all execution methods in the Roman Empire.

Chapter 4: 'When I am weak, I am strong': God's grace and the strength of weakness

1 Paul Tournier, *Medicina de la Persona*, Andamio-Clie, p. 167.

2 John R. W. Stott, *God's New Society: The Message of Ephesians*, IVP, 1979, p. 207.

Chapter 5: Angels along my path: the love that heals

1 John Stott, *The Contemporary Christian*, Inter-Varsity Press, Leicester, 1992, p. 148.

2 Helen Keller, *Light in My Darkness*, Chrysalis Books, Pennsylvania, 1994, p. 96. For a wider knowledge of this amazing deaf-mute and blind woman, see chapter 5.

3 The book *Tracing the Rainbow*, by Pablo Martinez, Authentic Media, 2004, provides further material for the reader interested in this subject. In particular we recommend chapter 3, 'How can we help?'. Although the book deals with the subject of bereavement and loss, when it comes to helping and comforting others there is much in common with the chronic pain of a thorn that often also entails loss and a bereavement process, which is why we consider the book a recommended accompaniment to this one.

4 Philip Yancey, *What is So Amazing about Grace?*, 1997, Zondervan Publishing House, Michigan, p. 15.

5 Quoted by Raymond Brown in *Christ Above All: The Message of Hebrews*, IVP, Leicester, 1982, p. 186.

6 Donald Guthrie, *Hebrews, Tyndale New Testament Commentaries*, Inter-Varsity Press, Leicester, 1983, p. 215.

7 This is how the Spanish Reina-Valera version of 1960 renders it: 'expert or experienced in suffering' (*La Santa Biblia*, Revisión de 1960, Versión de Casidoro de Reina y Cipriano de Valera, Sociedades Bíblicas de América Latina).

8 For a more exhaustive study of this topic I recommend two recent books: *Experiencing Healing Prayer: A Journey from Hurts to Wholeness* by Rick Richardson, Inter-Varsity Press, Leicester, 2005, and *Prayer: Does It Make Any Difference?* by Philip Yancey, Hodder and Stoughton, London, 2006.

9 This concept is developed fully in the book, *I and Thou*, by Martin Buber.

10 J. M. Martínez, *Abba, Father*, Editorial Clie, 1990, p. 25.

11 Richard Foster, *Celebration of Discipline*, Hodder and Stoughton, London, 1980, p. 30.

12 J. M. Lochman, *Unser Vater*, Gütersloh, 1988.

Chapter 6: Recovering the joy of living: new values for a different life

1 Jean Rostand, French biologist and writer, in his book *Humanly Possible*, quoted by C. Everett Koop, M.D., in *The Right to Live, The Right to Die*, Tyndale House Publishers, USA, 1976, p. 9.

2 Helen Keller, *Light in My Darkness*, Chrysalis Books, Pennsylvania, revised and edited by Ray Silverman, 1994, p. 118.

3 Ibid., p. 110.

4 William Barclay, *The Gospel of Matthew*, Vol. 1, Saint Andrew Press, Edinburgh, 1972, p. 84.

5 Os Guinness, *When No One Sees: The Importance of Character in an Age of Image*, The Trinity Forum Study Series, NavPress, 2000, p. 16.

6 Paul Tournier, *Creative Suffering*, SCM Press Ltd, London, 1982, p. 29.

7 Paul Tournier, ibid.

8 Quoted by John Stott, *Calling Christian Leaders*, InterVarsity Press, Leicester, 2002, p. 53.

9 Gaius Davies, *Genius, Grief and Grace*, Christian Focus Publications, Fearn, Ross-shire, Scotland, 2003.

10 Quoted from *The Comprehensive Textbook of Psychiatry*, H. Kaplan, 3rd edn, William and Wilkins, Baltimore, 1980, Vol. III, pp. 1510–1511.

11 John Stott, ibid., p. 56.

12 Dr Gaius Davies, ibid., p. 94.

13 James M. Gordon, *Evangelical Spirituality*, SPCK, London, 1982, 1991, p. 82.

14 Gene Edwards, *A Tale of Three Kings*, Christian Books, 1980, p. 33.

15 Miguel de Unamuno, quoted by Dr Pedro Laín Entralgo, *Esperanza en tiempos de crisis*, Galaxia Gutenberg, 1993, p. 65.

16 Helen Keller, ibid., p. 3.

17 P. Laín Entralgo, *Esperanza en tiempos de crisis*, Galaxia Gutenberg, 1993, p. 58.

18 Ibid., p. 65.

19 This is the third verse of his hymn 'God moves in a mysterious way'.

For more details of books published by IVP, visit our **website** where you will find all the latest information, including:

Book extracts
Author profiles and interviews
Reviews
Downloads
Online bookshop
Christian bookshop finder

You can also sign up for our **regular email newsletters** which are tailored to your particular interests, and tell others what you think about this book by posting a review.

We publish a wide range of books on various subjects, including:

Christian living
Key reference works
Bible commentary series
Small-group resources
Topical issues
Theological studies

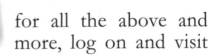

for all the above and more, log on and visit

www.ivpbooks.com